
The
War-Making Powers
of the
President

The War-Making Powers of the President

Constitutional and International
Law Aspects

Ann Van Wynen Thomas
A. J. Thomas, Jr.

Foreword by Charles O. Galvin

SMU PRESS • DALLAS

Library of Congress Cataloging in Publication Data

Thomas, Ann Van Wynen.
    The war-making powers of the president.

    Includes index.
    1. War and emergency powers—United States.
I. Thomas, A. J. (Aaron Joshua), 1918-   . II. Title.
KF5060.T48   1982   343.73′01   82-10541
ISBN 0-87074-185-3   347.3031

CONTENTS

FOREWORD

THE PRIVILEGE of writing this foreword is a great one indeed. The Doctors and Professors Thomas have been close friends and respected academic colleagues for a great many years. This latest work is another in a long series of books in which they have made a significant and substantial contribution to constitutional and international law.

In a complex representative democracy, who has the authority to commit the resources of the nation—its people and its material—to the declaration and the conduct of war? This inquiry is of utmost importance in these times, because the engagement of the nation in even limited hostilities in a nuclear age could portend its total destruction.

Who, then, has the authority? Congress has the power to declare war and to make appropriations for the support of the military forces, but the President is the Commander-in-Chief of the military forces. Suppose that a Congress declared war and provided for its support, and further suppose that a President—through ineptitude, neglect, or an unwillingness to engage in hostilities—appointed ineffectual military commanders and thus so intruded himself into the conduct of military affairs as to impede seriously the progress of the war and thus endanger the nation. On the other hand, suppose that the Congress refused to declare war or provide the resources for its prosecution, and further suppose that the President in his role as the Commander-in-Chief determined that the national security was so jeopardized as to require immediate and aggressive action.

In these cases the Constitution creates a dilemma which the experience of two hundred years has not fully resolved. Moreover, as recently as the era of our participation in the war in Vietnam, no institutional arrangements for the handling of the problem have been made clear. If war has not been declared, so long as the Executive and the Congress are in general concord about the need to engage in hostilities the courts will probably not interfere as a matter of political pragmatism. Yet if the Executive continued the engagement without congressional support, then a more serious difficulty would be presented. It could cease to be a matter of political concern and would become a constitutional challenge in the courts. Was the President acting in self-defense, or pursuant to treaty? Was he seeking to rescue American lives in danger, and in so doing did he engage the nation in prolonged and protracted hostilities?

It is to these most important concerns that the Thomases have addressed themselves. They have provided a historical, a critical, and an analytical treatise which is a major contribution in the field. Although they conclude that the power of the President to commit forces abroad remains a dark continent of American jurisprudence, their splendid work has illumined the subject to the benefit of all who search the area.

CHARLES O. GALVIN

School of Law
Southern Methodist University
November, 1982

INTRODUCTION

THE HISTORY OF THE UNITED STATES is fraught with controversy as to the competing powers of President and Congress to commit military forces abroad for the purpose of conducting hostilities. The controversy reached a climax during the Vietnam debacle, but even that dreary episode and the resulting congressional attempt to curb presidential power can hardly be said to have solved the constitutional dilemma. To those of simplistic mental bent the answer is crystal clear. The use of armed force abroad is a power granted to the Congress through that body's constitutional power to declare war. Nevertheless it should be pointed out that the Korean and Vietnam ventures, both major conflicts, were carried on with no congressional declaration of war. Moreover, considerably more than one hundred military ventures of lesser intensity have been conducted without congressional authorization.[1]

History then, if not the Constitution, would appear to justify what might be termed presidential war-making. Jurists, statesmen, and politicians have found constitutional justification for use of force abroad upon presidential initiative alone. The words of Senator Tom Connally support this viewpoint: "The authority of the President as Commander-in-Chief to send the armed forces to any place required by the security of the United States has often been questioned but never denied."[2]

At an earlier period in history William Howard Taft declared bluntly that Congress could not take away from the President "his power to determine the movements of the army and navy" so long as resort to their use was made "to defend the country against invasion, to suppress insurrection and to take care that the laws be faithfully executed."[3] Secretary of State Dean Acheson equated the President's power "with the carrying out of the broad foreign policy of the United States . . ." He also believed that "the authority may not be interfered with by Congress in the exercise of powers which it has under the Constitution."[4] Senator Goldwater has stated "that the President can take military action at any time he feels danger for the country, or stretching a point, for its position in the world."[5]

Thomas Jefferson would apparently disagree with such presidential prerogative. He said: "We have already given in example one effectual check to the Dog of War by transferring the power of letting him loose from the Executive to the Legislative body from those who are to spend to those who are to pay."[6] Abraham Lincoln as a young man in 1848 would agree with Jefferson. He believed that the Constitution gave the war-making power to Congress.[7] It should, however, be remembered that he ordered the use of armed force against the Confederacy prior to congressional declaration of war.[8]

Others have taken great issue with a broad presidential power to commit the nation to a use of force without congressional authority to do so. Senator Robert A. Taft refused to follow the beliefs of his father and expressed the view that the President had no constitutional power to commit American troops abroad without congressional authorization.[9] The Fulbright Committee opined in 1967 that

[e]xcepting only the necessary authority of the President to repel a sudden attack, the war power was vested in the Congress. Only in recent years has it passed to the executive, contributing to the dangerous tendency toward executive supremacy in foreign policy, a tendency which the committee hopes to see arrested and reversed.[10]

It is interesting to note that Senator Fulbright apparently did not share this view in 1961 when he wrote that "the President has full responsibility, which cannot be shared, for military decisions in a world in which the difference between safety and cataclysm can be a matter of hours or even minutes." [11]

Finally, it may be noted that there are those who believe that the power of the Congress versus the power of the President to commit American troops to a use of force against a foreign sovereign must, constitutionally speaking, remain in a gray or twilight area, inasmuch as the Constitution does not give us a clear-cut rule. As Arthur Schlesinger, Jr., has declared: "While the Constitution sets outer limits on both Presidential and Congressional action, it leaves a wide area of 'joint possession.' Common sense, therefore, argues for congressional participation as well as for Presidential responsibility in the great decisions of peace and war." [12]

Advocates of presidential war-making power advance many reasons for the existence and necessity of the prerogative. The executive power rests in one man, the legislative power in many. There is as a result a unity in the office of the presidency which makes it possible for the President to make up his mind and to act with dispatch and secrecy, factors which are regarded as essential in the delicate realm of foreign relations. Here speedy and purposeful action is often requisite to counter moves from abroad and to deal with rapidly changing international events. Congress, it is claimed, is too cumbersome and ponderous a body to meet and deal with foreign policy and foreign military complexities. Too, the President can negotiate and act secretly, and such secrecy is often demanded by the necessities of a challenge as to whether or not resort should be had to the use of the military. The President also has superior sources of information which permit him to act with full knowledge of the situation. He has foreign experts at his command, and the vast intelligence-gathering machinery is at his hand. As the case of *United States* v. *Curtiss-Wright Export Corporation* puts it:

Moreover, he, not Congress, has the better opportunity of knowing the conditions which prevail in foreign countries, and especially is this true in time of war. He has his confidential sources of information. He has his agents in the form of diplomatic, consular and other officials. Secrecy in respect of information gathered by them may be highly necessary, and the premature disclosure of it productive of harmful results. [13]

Moreover, the executive branch is always in session to deal with any emergencies which might occasion the use of armed force, whereas the houses of Congress are at times adjourned. The exigencies of a situation can well demand action when Congress may not be in session. Finally, it is argued that in reality most of our declared wars have begun and fighting has commenced prior to a congressional declaration of war; and even when such has not been the case the President through his conduct of foreign policy has made a declaration of war by Congress inevitable. Viewed in this light, the actual congressional declaration appears to be superfluous.

Detractors of presidential power dispute these claims. The need for urgent speedy action by the President is, they say, exaggerated. Most of the so-called emergency situations which have resulted in a presidential use of force have not in reality demanded immediate military action and military response. Indeed, delay for a wiser thinking through of the state of affairs might well have been advantageous to the nation and to the conduct of international affairs. Moreover, Congress has demonstrated on various occasions that it can act with dispatch when urgency is demanded. The declaration of war in World Wars I and II and the Gulf of Tonkin Resolution authorizing a use of force in Vietnam are instances cited to prove the point. On the other hand, the institutional unity of the office of President and the fact that the executive power is vested by the Constitution in one man do not necessarily make for speed, secrecy, and superior information. The executive branch of government is today large and unwieldly. It is often disunited as to the action necessary in the face of certain events. Leaks of official information in modern times demonstrate an ineptness in this branch to maintain secrecy. Too, there is nothing to prevent the President from sharing secret information in closed hearings with the Congress, the body in a democratic republican nation which should share in the vital information which might necessitate a use of armed force abroad and the decision to use the armed force. After all, it is contended, the people or their representatives in the Congress have a right to know of and share in decisions affecting the national security and the all-important issues of war and peace.

The idea that the President alone possesses the information and its sources through his control of the foreign policy apparatus and its experts is also subject to attack. Opposing thought would believe that the Congress can also gain information through congressional experts in the field of international and military affairs. After all, the Congress does have committees to assist it. And, as has been pointed out, there is no exclusivity in the executive as to the correctness of the information gathered or as to error in the use of such information once it is gathered. The fact that the President is always in session and the Congress is not is less important today. Times have changed. In these days of rapid communication and transportation, the Congress can be convened in short order so as to confer with the President. Delays in the convening of the Congress can hardly be considered a valid argument for presidential superiority.

Finally, as to the *fait accompli* postulate, it may be that hostilities ordered by the President have occurred before a declaration of war; still, this should not mean that the President should be permitted to conduct those hostilities for an indefinite period without congressional declaration. Moreover, the congressional power of war declaration was given by the Constitution, it is argued, so that Congress can be a valid component in the machinery of government to prevent the executive from acting in such a way as to plunge the country into war on his sole initiative and prerogative.[14]

To resolve this dispute between views of the powers of the Congress and the President, if indeed it will ever be satisfactorily resolved, an examination of the constitutional power of the President and the Congress which bear upon war-making and uses of force in foreign affairs to determine the proper constitutional assignment of power between the two becomes requisite. Our starting point, of course, should be the Constitution, and the meaning ascribed to its words to the extent that meaning can be derived from the words of the founding fathers.

ANN VAN WYNEN THOMAS
A. J. THOMAS, JR.

School of Law
Southern Methodist University
November, 1982

The
War-Making Powers
of the
President

1

THE FOUNDING FATHERS
AND THE CONSTITUTION

THE MEN WHO JOINED TOGETHER in Philadelphia in 1787 to draft
the Constitution of the United States were imbued with the idea that
a central or national government with strength and energy had become
necessary. For some ten years the nation had conducted its government
under the Articles of Confederation, a document which created a loose
confederation of states with a weak central government the powers of
which were exercised by the Congress.[1] This body exercised both legislative and executive power. There was no president, not even a prime
minister. Moreover, and in spite of the fact that the former thirteen
colonies were desperately trying to establish a permanent independence
through force of arms, when they adopted the Articles of Confederation
they were unwilling to commit themselves to standing armies or to give
to the central government strong war powers. Article VII prohibited
the states from establishing a permanent military force in times of
peace "except as in the Judgment of the United States in Congress
assembled" it should be necessary for "the defense of the state."[2] On the
other hand, the states were required to keep a well-regulated and disci-
plined militia "sufficiently armed and accoutered."[3]

States were also forbidden to engage in any war without the consent of the Congress unless actually invaded by an enemy or in case of an imminent invasion which would not admit of delay.[4] The power of "determining on peace and war" was lodged exclusively with the central government, but this power was limited by the fact that nine states must consent to engagement in war.[5]

If they did consent, Congress could then declare war and enlist volunteers in an army, but it had to requisition from the states the money to equip and supply this army. It could request the use of the state's civilian militia to fight enemies internal and external, but there was no guarantee that one state would come to the aid of another or to the aid of all. Shays's rebellion in Massachusetts in 1786-87 highlighted the desperate need for a stronger national military authority. Most of the Massachusetts militiamen were sympathetic with the rebels, and neither the central government nor the governments of the neighboring states were able or willing speedily to aid the government of Massachusetts in putting down the revolt.[6] Reform became inevitable, for the rebellion indicated that the confederation could be defeated by enemies within as well as without.

When the delegates to the Constitutional Convention gathered, they were tired of ineffectual government under the Articles of Confederation and were willing to concede more powers to the national government.[7] Although the Constitution which emerged is a short document, uses words sparingly, and is an outline of government, still the external powers of the nation inclusive of the military powers are largely to be exercised by the federal government, and those powers are shared in varying degree between the Congress and the President. Nevertheless there was much debate and disagreement concerning these powers in the efforts of the framers to balance authority and liberty.

Among the primary questions concerning strengthened national powers were those having to do with military arrangement. George Washington believed that the military experience of the Revolution proved America's need for a professional national army. To him the state civilian militia was simply unequal to the exigencies of offensive or defensive large-scale warfare. But many of those at the Constitutional Convention disagreed. Mason, for example, sought to assure the liberties of the people against "the danger of standing armies in time of peace."[8] Even James Madison agreed that since peacetime armies "are allowed on all hands to be evil, it is well to discountenance them by the constitution, as far as will consist with the essential power of the government. . . ."[9] Elbridge Gerry of Massachusetts sought by various means to limit both the size of the army and the degree of control to be exercised by the Congress over the state militias. On one occasion he tried to limit the numbers of troops to be kept in time of peace to two thousand, or three thousand at the most.[10] This suggestion brought forth the only unneutral remark from Chairman Washington, when in an audible aside he whispered to the deaf and aging Ben Franklin that in such a case it would be well to include also in the Constitution a stipulation that no enemy would be allowed to attack the United States with a larger force.[11]

Pinckney argued that the Constitution should contain words making the military always subordinate to the civil power and that the dangers which might arise from an entrenched permanent military force could be alleviated by a prohibition upon the legislative branch from granting money for the support of military land forces for more than one year.[12] The idea found a place in the Constitution, but the one-year limitation was increased to a two-year period.[13] It might be noted that this two-year limitation on appropriations did not apply to the naval forces, which were seen as a permanent necessity to a country whose main potential enemies were overseas.[14]

Concurrent with the argument over the standing army was the debate over who should have the control of the army, including the power to declare or make war. Hamilton at first suggested that the Senate alone should have the sole war-declaring power,[15] to which Pinckney agreed because the Senate would be better acquainted with foreign affairs than the House of Representatives and inasmuch as it was to be a smaller body it would be better equipped to make a decision.[16] Randolph of Virginia disagreed and declared that the power to declare war should be placed in the House of Representatives, for this organ represented the people of the nation instead of the states.[17] The Constitution originally provided that the senators were elected by the legislatures of the various states.[18] Butler, following the English practice, argued that the power should be vested in the executive.[19] In that nation power over foreign relations, war powers, and treaties was exercised by the king.[20] Butler declared that the power "to make war should be vested in the President who will have all the requisite qualities and will not make war but when the nation will support it."[21] Hamilton then modified his original stand and said that perhaps the President should have the power to make war with the advice of the Senate.[22] A compromise between the Pinckney and Randolph views was finally obtained, in which the whole of Congress was to be involved in making war. In the draft of this provision which was given to the Convention on August 6, 1787, Congress was given the power to "make" war. This verb, however, was later changed after some discussion so that Congress was empowered to "declare" war. This weakened the original language and has caused debate throughout the ensuing years. The reason for the change, as stated by James Madison, lay in recognition of the fact that the executive power might be needed to repel sudden attacks.[23]

Thus we find that Congress has the sole power to declare war, leaving this decision not with the military or its civilian head, the President as Commander-in-Chief, but with the elected representatives of the people. The President as chief executive was to be responsible for the enforcement of all laws.[24] He was given a major share of the responsibility for the conduct of foreign relations as Commander-in-Chief of the army and navy and of the state militia when it was called into the service of the United States.[25]

It was also recognized that the treaty-making power had concealed in it a capacity to commit American armed forces to the support of foreign alliances. Strong debate emerged as to where this power should be lodged. If the President were made Commander-in-Chief, Madison asserted, he would necessarily derive so much power and importance from a state of war that he might be tempted, if he had the exclusive treaty-making power, to impede a treaty of peace. To Madison the treaty-making power should require a concurrence of two-thirds of the Senate.[26] The Committee on Detail would place the power in the Senate alone,[27] while others thought that if the Congress were to be given the power to declare war this body alone should have the power to make treaties.[28] Gerry believed that a majority of the Senate was much more liable to be corrupted by an enemy than the whole legislative body.[29] Madison argued that a distinction should be made between different types of treaties. The President and Senate should be allowed to make treaties of alliance for limited terms, while the concurrence of the whole legislature should be required for all other treaties.[30]

At one point Madison believed that the concurrence of two-thirds of the senators should not be necessary for peace treaties, which should be allowed to be made with less difficulty than other treaties.[31] To this Wilson agreed, stating that if two-thirds are necessary to make peace the minority may perpetuate the war against the sense of the majority.[32] But Gerry pointed out that in treaties of peace the nation's interests, such as fisheries, territory, etc., were at stake, and these might be sacrificed in a peace treaty. Therefore, more than a simple majority should be required.[33] In the long run it was merely agreed that the President was to have the power to negotiate the treaties as a check against Senate action, but the right of approval of treaties was reserved to two-thirds of the Senate as a check upon executive action.[34]

Like much of the Constitution, the resulting clauses dealing with the military were compromise solutions based on a system of checks and balances. Congress was given the power to levy and collect taxes for the common defense to raise and support armies, and to establish rules for their discipline, but the states retained their historic militias and the right to appoint their militia officers. If the need should arise for more manpower than existed in the national army, the federal government could call into national service the state militias; but this service was limited to the suppression of insurrection, the repelling of invasion, or the execution of the nation's laws.[35] The President had the power to commission national military officers, but this was checked by the fact that his choices were subjected to the advice and consent of the Senate.[36] The power to declare war was lodged in the whole Congress subject to presidential veto.[37] Nevertheless, it was recognized that the chief executive officer of the nation would be responsible for the conduct of foreign relations in peace as well as in war. Hence the President was made the commander of all of the armed forces, including the militia when in the service of the United States.[38] This arrangement had the virtue of strengthening civilian control but at the same time provided a unified command. A further cloak against possible military despotism existed in the injunction that Congress could make no military appropriations for a period longer than two years.

In granting power in such a way to rival departments of government, a constitutional built-in conflict was bound to emerge, and it would seem that the framers expected such conflict. Particularly is this true when one considers that the Congress has the power to declare war, but the President as Commander-in-Chief has the supreme command and direction of the military forces. Obviously when Congress declares war the Commander-in-Chief directs and controls these armed forces in its conduct. But is he so limited in his power? Although he may not declare war, does the Constitution permit him to make war, or perhaps to use force short of war as Commander-in-Chief? It has been so stated, but just as vehemently denied.[39] The language of the Constitution is ambiguous. Nor does the intent of the framers emerge from their debates with the clarity which might be desired. Perhaps the language of the constitutional debates would indicate that a larger portion of the war power was to be placed in the Congress, and insofar as the United States is concerned that body through its power to declare war would be empowered to initiate war. The President would be left free to repel sudden attacks. But what is meant by sudden attacks? Moreover, no clear-cut answer is to be found to the question of the President's power to use force short of war.

Light may be shed on this enigma through consideration of the practices of the executive and legislative branches with respect to the uses of military force abroad throughout the history of the nation. After all, the Constitution is only an outline of government. Its lacunae may be filled in by the governmental practices which take place within its word boundaries. Experiences in accommodating this living document to the vicissitudes of history become important in determining its meaning, for the interpretations of constitutions do respond to changing historical concepts of political and social values, and historical practices do shape the meaning of the Constitution if not violative of its language or of the clear-cut intent of its framers.[40]

2

PRESIDENTIAL USE OF FORCE
1789-1900

FROM THE EARLIEST DAYS of the Republic, as we have seen, debate has occurred as to the powers of the President and Congress *vis-à-vis* the power to initiate war and to use force.[1] In 1798 George Washington proclaimed the neutrality of the United States in the war which was taking place between Britain and France.[2] Neutrality pertained to a non-use of force and not to war or a use of force; nevertheless, serious controversy prevailed as to Washington's power to issue such a proclamation. As there was no explicit grant in the Constitution on this subject, the argument for presidential power was based primarily upon executive prerogative to make and carry out foreign policy.

Hamilton defended executive authority, contending that foreign policy belonged to the executive even though the consequences of the conduct of foreign policy might affect congressional power to declare war. He held to the view that the first sentence of Article II of the Constitution vested the executive power in the President, and that such grant was restricted only by the qualifications and exceptions stipulated in other sections of the Constitution. Implicit in the Hamiltonian argument was the assumption, quite correctly drawn from British precedent, that the war-declaring and treaty-making powers are executive in nature. Under British practice such powers were placed in the crown. The qualifications imposed upon these powers by the Constitution of the United States did not change the essential nature of the powers, but altered their exercise only. Since the power to declare neutrality was an executive power, and since its exercise was not limited or curtailed by the Constitution, the power remained within the presidential prerogative. Moreover, to Hamilton, the presidential power to proclaim neutrality did not detract from the congressional power to declare war.[3]

Madison, on the other hand, could not agree. To him, presidential proclamations of neutrality invaded the congressional authority to declare war, for the congressional power preempted not only the power to initiate war, but also all problems of peace and war.[4]

Although Washington did issue the neutrality proclamation, early Presidents were cautious when it came to the initiation of hostilities abroad and were respectful of the congressional war-making authority. The years 1798-1800 were to see the United States engaged in an undeclared naval war against France caused by French interference with United States shipping. Although there was never a formal congressional declaration of war, still the conflict was not one waged by unilateral presidential action. The Congress in a series of acts in effect authorized an imperfect limited war. The Supreme Court later held such authorization to be within the congressional power.[5]

A resort to naval force occurred in 1801, this time against the Barbary pirates and upon the orders of President Jefferson. When Congress reconvened, Jefferson obtained congressional authorization for offensive and defensive military activities.[6] Hamilton believed that once a foreign power makes war on the United States as the Barbary pirates had done, then the nation is automatically at war, and a declaration by the Congress is no longer necessary and is nugatory.[7]

The first declared war engaged in by the United States was the War of 1812. Although Madison at an earlier time had contended that the executive would be more disposed than Congress to make war,[8] the facts proved otherwise to a degree at this time in history, for it was a belligerent faction in the Congress which demanded war with Britain.[9] Madison acceded and the war was instituted by formal congressional declaration.

In 1815, Madison, like Jefferson, obtained authorization from the Congress to engage in limited warfare against Algeria;[10] but later, in

1817, President Monroe failed to consult Congress when he sent forces under Andrew Jackson into Florida to chastise marauders, Seminole Indians, who were raiding into United States territory. It was claimed that there was a right to pursue an enemy in the right of self-defense and that defensive acts of hostility could be authorized by the President alone.[11]

During the remainder of the nineteenth century the Presidents were to become bolder. There were many instances of the use of unauthorized force by the chief executive. Force was used to suppress piracy and the slave trade, in hot pursuit of criminals across the borders into other states, and to protect American lives and property in foreign states in instances when law and order had broken down in those states.[12] Such uses of force, in general authorized by international law, came to be recognized in practice as constitutionally permissible even though the power was not expressly delegated to the President by the Constitution.[13]

Three wars occurred during this period. Two were commenced without congressional authorization or declaration. In 1846, after the annexation of Texas, President Polk ordered American troops into disputed territory between Mexico and Texas. After attack by Mexican troops, the American armed forces destroyed the Mexican forces. The President requested of the Congress that war not be declared, but that the existence of war be recognized. This the Congress did.[14] John Quincy Adams, in heated opposition, stated that the war had never been declared but only recognized as being in existence because of Mexico's attack which was "a notorious violation of the truth."[15] This situation has been noted as one where the President provoked the war and simply presented the Congress with a *fait accompli* to which it was forced to accede. The Congress did later censure the President's action by a statement which called the war "unnecessary and unconstitutionally begun by the President of the United States."[16] Abraham Lincoln, then a member of the House of Representatives, stated his opposition to presidential war-making:

Allow the President to invade a neighboring nation whenever he shall deem it necessary to repel an invasion, and you allow him to do so whenever he may choose to say he deems it necessary for such a purpose, and you allow him to make war at his pleasure. Study to see if you can fix any limit to his power in this respect, after having given him so much power as you propose. . . .[17]

Despite this language by Representative Lincoln in speaking of the

Mexican War, President Lincoln saw fit to use force in order to suppress the South's attempt at secession and to put down what he considered an illegal rebellion. He acted as Commander-in-Chief and under his power to execute laws. At a later time, Congress was requested to ratify and recognize these emergency actions taken to save the nation, and such congressional ratification was forthcoming.[18]

The Spanish American War was initiated by a joint resolution of the Congress which was an ultimatum ordering Spain to withdraw from Cuba and to relinquish its sovereignty over that island. The President was authorized to use force to carry out the terms of the resolution. Spain severed diplomatic relations and began hostilities. Congress then declared war. This war was largely instigated by Congress. The belligerent emotions of its members had been aroused by the sinking of the battleship *Maine* and a journalistic crusade for war.[19]

3

EXPANSION OF PRESIDENTIAL POWER
1900 TO WORLD WAR II

PRESIDENTIAL INITIATIVE in the use of force without congressional declaration of war or authorization was to become marked in the twentieth century. At the turn of the century in 1900 President McKinley sent five thousand troops to China to join an international army in order to put down the Boxer Rebellion.[1] The Chinese government had been unable or unwilling to quell the uprising, which was directed against foreigners who had been subjected to Boxer depredations. Foreign legations in China had also been attacked. The United States forces were sent in to protect the legations, to rescue American officials and other Americans in danger, and to protect the lives and properties of Americans in China and all legitimate American interests. This intervention led to a declaration of war by China against the United States. The United States Congress did not see fit to reciprocate with its own declaration.[2]

Presidential authorization of a use of armed force occurred again in 1903. After the Senate of Colombia failed to ratify a treaty with the United States for the construction of an interoceanic canal across the Isthmus of Panama, Panama rebelled against Colombia, then its mother country.[3] In the civil strife that followed, the United States intervened by means of a naval force to thwart Colombia's suppression of the rebellious province. This force prevented the landing of Colombian forces in the area, thus effectively preventing the quashing of the revolt. Immediately thereafter, the United States accorded Panama recognition as an independent nation.[4] President Theodore Roosevelt sought justification of his action by pointing to certain treaty rights with Colombia, the national interest and the safety of the United States, and the collective interests of the civilized world.[5] He later boasted that he took the Isthmus, stating, ". . . I took the Canal Zone and let Congress debate, and while the debate goes on the Canal also."[6]

Following this episode, presidential military intervention in the Caribbean area was to become almost endemic.[7] After the Spanish American War, the United States disclaimed intention to annex Cuba.[8] Nevertheless Cuban independence was impaired through the Platt Amendment which was incorporated into the treaty of 1903-4 between Cuba and the United States.[9] Among other things it provided:

That the government of Cuba consents that the United States may exercise the right to intervene for the preservation of Cuban independence, the maintenance of a government adequate for the protection of life, property, and individual liberty and for discharging the obligations with respect to Cuba imposed by the Treaty of Paris on the United States, now to be assumed and undertaken by the government of Cuba.[10]

Thereafter, and in accord with the terms of the agreement, the President of the United States on various occasions ordered the landing of small armed contingents to maintain a government in Cuba adequate for the protection of life, property, and individual liberties. These interventions usually took place when rebellion, civil strife, and disorder in Cuba threatened stable government in that country.[11] They continued until the United States right of intervention was renounced during the Franklin D. Roosevelt administration.

Woodrow Wilson, a President remembered for his efforts on behalf of world peace, felt called upon to resort to a use of armed force on many differing occasions. With the overthrow of President Porfirio Diaz and the outbreak of the great revolution in Mexico in 1911, relations between the United States and Mexico became far from amicable. When Wilson came into power he found General Victoriano Huerta in power as President of Mexico. Huerta was regarded by Wilson as a usurper.

Thus Wilson refused to recognize the Huerta regime on the ground that Huerta had seized office unconstitutionally by force and had murdered his predecessor in office, Madero.[12] Wilson not only failed to recognize the Huerta government but also revoked the embargo on arms shipments to Mexico so that Huerta's opposition, led by Carranza, could more quickly oust Huerta by revolutionary means.[13]

This later action, plus the failure to recognize the regime, created bitterness in the Huerta government, with the result that United States sailors were arrested by local politicians in Tampico and Vera Cruz. They were released by Huerta, who expressed regret but refused to comply with a demand made by the United States admiral in charge and upheld by President Wilson that a formal salute of twenty-one guns be given. Because of this refusal, President Wilson was determined to order a pacific blockade of the Mexican coast and an occupation of the port of Vera Cruz. But before so doing he asked Congress to authorize the use of land and naval forces.[14] In his request he was careful to state his position:

No doubt I could do what is necessary in the circumstances to enforce respect for our government without recourse to the Congress and yet not exceed my constitutional powers as President; but I do not wish to act in a matter possible of so grave consequence except in close conference and cooperation with both the Senate and the House. I, therefore, come to ask your approval that I should use the armed forces of the United States in such ways and to such extent as may be necessary.[15]

After Huerta's fall from power United States forces were withdrawn from Vera Cruz, but disorder continued in Mexico. Francisco Villa, a revolutionary chieftan, murdered a group of citizens of the United States in Mexico and also conducted a series of raids into the United States. These raids prompted the President to dispatch into Mexico a United States force under the command of General Pershing in "hot pursuit" of the bandits.[16]

At the turn of the century, the Dominican Republic found itself in a not unusual state of political chaos, revolution, and counterrevolution. As a consequence the nation had failed to make payment of debts owed to creditors in the United States and certain European countries. To forestall European interventions to collect such debts, the United States obtained from the Dominican Republic an agreement which placed the bankrupt state in the hands of an American receiver who was empowered to handle the nation's finances to secure payment to foreign creditors.[17] A treaty between the United States and the Dominican Republic later granted the former the right to protect the receiver general and his assistants in the performance of their duties.[18] In 1916, in the face of revolutionary activities, President Wilson ordered a military occupation of the Dominican Republic based upon the violation of the treaty. This occupation was to last until 1924.[89]

In Haiti a similar presidential military occupation took place, also as a result of disorder and civil strife. In 1915 a reign of terror existed in that country. President Wilson ordered an armed intervention to protect the lives and properties of citizens of the United States and other foreigners, particularly those of British and French nationality. Intimations had come to the President that if he did not act to bring about an end to the anarchy and turbulence those European nations would do so. Moreover there was some fear of German influence and a possible German take-over of the island. Thus, in order to prevent an extension of European hegemony over the strategic Caribbean territory, the United States intervened. A treaty was later signed with Haiti which, among other things, granted to the United States a right to intervene for the preservation of Haitian independence and the maintenance of a government adequate for the protection of life, property, and liberty. Thereafter for something like two decades Haiti remained a protectorate of the United States.[20]

As early as 1854, a small United States force was ordered to Greytown, Nicaragua, by the secretary of the navy to protect the persons and property of American citizens against mob action. Certain property of an American company was destroyed by the town authorities. The United States minister to Nicaragua was assaulted. The naval commander was instructed by the President to obtain reparation for the losses to the company and for the indignity suffered by the minister. After a demand for apologies and reparations, and when none were forthcoming, the town was bombed by the navy, and a landing party burned it.[21] After the construction of the Panama Canal the United States became especially interested in promoting stability in the region near the canal for fear that internal disorder and internecine warfare might so endanger foreign lives, property, and investment as to give rise to foreign European intervention which, once effected, would endanger the isthmus. In 1909, when revolution occurred in Nicaragua, President Taft ordered marines into Nicaragua ostensibly to protect American lives and property.[22] Again in 1912 marines were landed, this time upon the request of the President of Nicaragua, when revolution threatened. By 1913 order of a sort was restored, and all were withdrawn except a hundred marines left as a legation guard.[23] Revolutionary disturbances were to cause a return of the marines in 1927, and by 1928 some 5,480 men were stationed in Nicaragua. President Coolidge explained that the action was taken to protect United States lives, property, investments, and business interests, to stop the turmoil which placed in jeopardy the rights granted by Nicaragua for the construction of a canal in that country, and to contribute to the stability of all Central America.[24] It was not until 1933 that the last of the United States marines were withdrawn from Nicaragua.

These earlier years of the twentieth century, at least until the coming into power of President Franklin D. Roosevelt, were days of American imperialistic ideas and of dollar diplomacy. But they were also days of crusading goodwill to right the world's ills, to end revolutionary conditions and dictatorships, and to force democratic processes abroad. The Congress for the most part was content with presidential developments abroad, including the forays into foreign nations with armed force to protect what were proclaimed to be American interests and rights.

Congress did fulfill its role in the initiation of war in 1918 when President Wilson requested from the Congress a declaration of war which brought about United States participation in World War I. However, he had previously armed and authorized American merchantmen to fire on sight, in view of Germany's policy of unrestricted submarine warfare.[25] The President was not concerned with congressional authorization when he committed United States forces to armed intervention into Russian territory in 1918, first in Archangel and vicinity and later in Siberia. The first expedition came after the Russian armistice with Germany. It was taken to bring about an allied junction with certain Czechoslovak troops and to prevent large amounts of war materials from falling into German hands. This action can be described as a command decision on a strategical maneuver which was an incident of the larger war effort against Germany; but the expedition did enter a new theater of war, and it came into armed contact with Russian bolsheviks. The Siberian venture was taken to maintain the balance of power in the Far East, primarily to prevent Japan from occupying large areas of Siberia and Manchuria following the collapse of Russian authority in the area. The President was strongly condemned for these expeditions, and particularly for maintaining U.S. troops in Russia following the armistice.[26]

A period of United States isolationism came into being after World War I, and the United States interventions, except in the Caribbean area, came to a halt. This was not to last. World War II was thrust upon the United States by the Japanese attack on Pearl Harbor, and following the fateful December 7 attack the Congress declared war. Nevertheless, prior to that time President Roosevelt had committed the United States to a course which could hardly be described as neutral in relation to the Axis powers. He did in fact authorize an undeclared naval war with Germany without congressional authorization when he ordered the navy to fire upon Axis vessels in American defensive waters. He swapped United States destroyers to the British for bases in the Americas by executive agreement. The military occupation of Greenland and Iceland was done in agreement with Denmark and Iceland respectively.[27] These and other actions favoring Britain over Germany and the Axis have caused certain commentators to remark that the congressional declaration of war was simply a recognition of a war which in reality was brought about by the President and his conduct of foreign policy.[28]

4

THE COLD WAR: DETENTE AND BEYOND

IF ONE HAD BEEN BLESSED with extrasensory perception when standing upon the threshold year following World War II one would have exclaimed "You ain't seen nothing yet!" in regard to future unilateral presidential uses of force in comparison with such uses previous to World War II. The cold war came into being because of the attempts on the part of the Soviet Union to advance Soviet imperialism by any means—threats, subversion, and force. In countering such Soviet expansionism, the United States faced problems of great magnitude in the conduct of American foreign policy, so that the government seemed to stagger from crisis to crisis. The management of foreign policy and the facing of crises were largely left to presidential prerogative and judgment, and in taking action to meet a crisis the President often acted in his role as Commander-in-Chief.

In June, 1950, the United States and the world were faced with the first major effort to effectuate the collective security system which the United Nations Charter had sought to establish. This occurred when North Korean troops swept into South Korea. To meet this breach of the peace the United Nations Security Council demanded a cessation of hostilities and a withdrawal of North Korean forces. All members of the United Nations were also urged to assist South Korea and to refrain from aiding North Korea.[1] A short time later, a resolution was passed calling upon members to provide military forces to a unified command under the United States.[2]

In November, 1950, the Korean action became enlarged when the Chinese Communists entered the fray on the side of North Korea. At this time the General Assembly of the United Nations called the Chinese intervention an aggression, affirmed the determination of the United Nations to continue the Korean action to meet that aggression, and called upon all states to continue to lend every assistance to the United Nations' action in Korea.[3]

Three days after the initial attack by North Korea and two days after the decision of the Security Council recommending that the member states render assistance to South Korea, the United States committed its armed forces to fight in Korea. President Truman was of the belief that if this aggression went unchallenged the world would face another world war. This so-called police action was to last much longer and was to involve the commitment of more men and war material than had been foreseen. Prolongation of the affair became inevitable when the Chinese Communists entered the war. Actually the Korean action was to last three years and at a cost of more than 140,000 casualties. Despite the magnitude of the conflict, congressional authorization for the sending of United States forces into battle was never sought. Nor was congressional authorization ever forthcoming.[4]

President Truman never doubted his constitutional authority to contribute United States forces to a United Nations peace-keeping effort. He was acting in accordance with the United Nations Charter—a treaty and the supreme law of the land—as well as with resolutions of United Nations organs taken in conformity with that Charter. Administration spokesmen also cited the President's powers in the field of foreign affairs and as Commander-in-Chief as constitutional authority.[5]

Shortly after President Truman had ordered American troops to intervene, the Department of State, acting as executive spokesman, issued a statement basing Truman's authority not solely on the United Nations resolutions and the treaty relationship, but primarily upon the presidential constitutional powers:

The President, as Commander-in-Chief of the Armed Forces of the United

States, has full control over the use thereof. He also has authority to conduct the foreign relations of the United States. Since the beginning of the United States history, he has, on numerous occasions, utilized these powers in sending armed forces abroad.[6]

After citing past instances of presidential use of armed force in the broad interests of American foreign policy, the administration asserted that there was a "traditional power of the President to use the Armed Forces of the United States without consulting Congress."[7]

Although Truman did consult informally with certain key members of Congress after the fact, it is nevertheless clear that he acted on his combined presidential powers plus his power to faithfully execute the international agreements of the United States.

Actually the Truman administration claimed that the dispatch of troops abroad by the President was an unlimited presidential prerogative, for some time later (and in a different context) Truman's secretary of state, Dean Acheson, testifying before the Senate Committees on Foreign Relations and Armed Services, flatly declared:

Not only has the President the authority to use the armed forces in carrying out the broad foreign policy of the United States and implementing treaties, *but it is equally clear that this authority may not be interfered with by the Congress in the exercise of powers which it* has under the Constitution. [Emphasis added][8]

Nevertheless, criticism was directed at the President for his failure to obtain congressional authorization. Senator Taft labeled the sending of troops to Korea, even though based upon a United Nations resolution, an undeclared war and a usurpation of authority. Moreover, he was of the opinion that the President had no power "without congressional approval to send troops to one country to defend it against a possible attack by another country."[9]

Attention was also called to the fact that presidential power had been limited by the Congress in that approval of Congress was required by that body whenever United States armed forces were to be placed at United Nations disposal in pursuance of a Security Council resolution. This had been stipulated in the United Nations Participation Act of 1945. It was alleged that both the Constitution and a United States statute had been ignored by the President.[10]

This debate concerning presidential power was to intensify when in late 1950 the President announced his intention to reinforce the American army in Europe in support of NATO. This reinforcement was to be made without reference to the Congress. A resolution was introduced which declared it to be the sense of Congress that additional forces were not to be sent abroad without prior congressional authorization. President Truman answered that he did not require congressional approval to send troops to Europe or anywhere else in the world. He claimed that his authority rested upon the Constitution's commander-in-chief clause. A resolution was finally adopted by the Senate which approved the deploying of troops to Europe, but at the same time sought to prohibit any additional forces without congressional approval.[11]

And Truman did not seek permission from Congress, in the last days of his administration, to send U-2 surveillance flights over the Eastern Mediterranean to check on the Anglo-French buildup which led to the Suez crisis of October-November, 1956.[12]

In spite of the Truman precedent, President Eisenhower was somewhat more considerate of the role of Congress in committing extensive numbers of American armed forces into situations where widespread hostilities might occur. In 1955, he sought congressional authorization for the use of American troops to protect the Chiang Kai-shek government on Taiwan in its possession of the Pescadores against the forces of the communist Chinese. In that request he stated his view:

Authority for some of the actions which might be required would be inherent in the authority of the Commander-in-Chief. Until Congress can act, I would not hesitate, so far as my constitutional powers extend, to take whatever emergency action might be forced upon us in order to protect the rights and security of the United States.

However, a suitable congressional resolution would clearly and publicly establish the authority of the President as Commander-in-Chief to employ the Armed Forces of this nation promptly and effectively for the purposes indicated if in his judgment it became necessary.[13]

This resolution passed easily, although Senator Wayne Morse complained that Congress could not delegate its power to declare war.[14] Speaker Sam Rayburn disagreed, believing that the President had the power to act without congressional authorization and consultation and that the resolution might be a dangerous precedent in limiting the powers of the Commander-in-Chief.[15]

In 1957 the President requested an authorization to provide military assistance to nations in the Middle East. A resolution embodying what came to be known as the Eisenhower Doctrine was enacted by the Congress. It recognized the fact that the United States "regards as vital to the national interest and world peace the preservation of the independence and integrity of the nations of the Middle East." It then stated:

To this end if the President determines the necessity thereof, the United States is prepared to use armed forces to assist any such nation or group of such nations requesting assistance against armed aggression from any country controlled by international communism.[16]

In 1958 President Eisenhower felt called upon to act in the Middle East. He ordered military forces into Lebanon without seeking further congressional approval and without specifically basing his authority on the 1957 Middle East Resolution. He said that the troops were sent "to protect American lives—there are about 2,500 Americans in Lebanon— and by their presence there to assist the Government of Lebanon to preserve its territorial integrity and political independence." He added, "I have come to the sober and clear conclusion that the action taken was essential to the welfare of the United States. It was required to support the principles of justice upon which peace and a stable international order depend."[17]

Also, even as President Truman before him, President Eisenhower sent U-2 flights over Russian and Cuba without seeking congressional approval. Nor did he seek such approval for the dispatch of certain military advisers to Southeast Asia.[18]

President Kennedy continued the U-2 surveillances without going to Congress, and he reluctantly permitted on his own authority the use of naval and air transport for the ill-fated Bay of Pigs mission.[19]

During the first hours of the missile crisis with Cuba in 1962, Kennedy rejected all suggestions of reconvening Congress or requesting a formal declaration of war.[20] He dispatched the U.S. naval forces in the so-called "quarantine" of Cuba, "acting under and by virtue of the authority conferred upon me by the Constitution and statutes of the United States Congress and the Organ of Consultation of the American Republics and to defend the security of the United States. . . ."[21] The resolution of Congress referred to by Kennedy had been passed a month before the Cuban missile crisis and the quarantine proclamation. The Cuban resolution contained no grant of authority to the President; it simply declared that the United States was determined to use any means necessary to prevent Cuba from extending its subversive activities throughout the hemisphere and from creating or using an externally supported military capacity which would endanger United States security.[22]

President Kennedy announced that surveillance of Cuba gave uncontrovertible evidence that the Soviet Union

under a cloak of secrecy and deception was converting the island into a potentially offensive nuclear base against the United States and the whole of the Western Hemisphere by rushing to completion offensive missile sites capable of launching both medium range and intermediate range ballistic missiles capable of carrying nuclear warheads, as well as by basing in Cuba jet bombers also capable of nuclear weapons.[23]

These actions were viewed as "an explicit threat to the peace and security of all the Americas, in flagrant and deliberate defiance of the Rio pact of 1947, the traditions of this nation and hemisphere . . . and the Charter of the United Nations." President Kennedy sought and obtained a resolution from the Organization of American States under the Rio Treaty which recommended that the member states, in accordance with that treaty,

take all measures, individually and collectively, including the use of armed force, which they may deem necessary to insure that the Government of Cuba cannot continue to receive from the Sino-Soviet powers military material and related supplies which may threaten the peace and security of the Continent and to prevent the missiles in Cuba with offensive capability from ever becoming an active threat to the peace and security to the Continent.[24]

After the approval of this resolution, the United States issued a proclamation entitled "Interdiction of the Delivery of Offensive Weapons to Cuba." Stating that he was acting "under the Constitution and laws of the United States, the Joint Resolution of Congress . . . and the resolution of the OAS," the President ordered interdicted the delivery of offensive weapons and associated materials to Cuba by the land, sea, and air forces of the United States.[25]

Although Kennedy cited the laws of the United States and the congressional resolution in part as the basis of the naval quarantine, there is evidence which suggests that he also believed in the constitutional power of the President to use force abroad.[26] Theodore Sorensen wrote that in the Cuban missile crisis the President acted by "executive order, Presidential proclamation and inherent powers, not under any resolution or act of Congress."[27]

Furthermore, President Kennedy never sought congressional approval when he introduced the first substantial numbers of American troops into Southeast Asia in 1962.[28]

In 1964 the United States, under orders of President Johnson, joined with Belgium to commit armed intervention in the Congo in order to rescue hostages who were citizens of at least eighteen foreign countries, including diplomatic officials who were being held and subjected to inhuman treatment by certain rebel forces engaged in civil strife. In addition to the justification of self-defense, i.e., the responsibility of the United States and Belgium to protect the lives of their own nationals, certain other grounds of legality were set forth, such as humanitarian intervention to save the lives of innocent nonnationals and the right of legation. It may be noted that the established government of the Congo requested the intervention.[29]

The year 1965 was to see another extensive presidential armed intervention. This use of armed force took place in the Dominican Republic and was occasioned by a revolutionary situation there which quickly led to chaos in the capital city and which caused fear of a communist take-over of the country à la Castro's Cuba. The antirebel military junta admitted to the authorities of the United States Embassy in Santo Domingo that it was unable to cope effectively with the threat posed by the action of the mobs and/or the rebel forces, and consequently it could no longer guarantee the safety of the citizens of the United States or of other foreign nations.[30] It therefore requested the assistance of United States military personnel for this purpose.[31] On April 28, in response to this request, the President of the United States ordered the landing of four hundred marines on Dominican soil "to give protection to hundreds of Americans who [were] still in the Dominican Republic and to escort them safely back to this country."[32] The same assistance was offered to the nationals of other states.

The following day the President made the decision to reinforce the original contingent by sending in additional troops. The United States forces were rapidly augmented until a troop buildup of something in excess of twenty thousand had taken place. Among the objectives for these landings were the quelling of bloodshed and the restoration of order. But the primary motive for the sending of such a large force was to prevent a communist take-over of the Dominican Republic. The enlarged military presence was said to be necessary "in view of the clear and present danger of the forcible seizure of power by the Communists."[33]

A few days later the President stressed the peace-keeping objectives of the action, explaining that it was an exercise of the presidential power to preserve the security of the hemisphere in accordance with the principles enunciated in the OAS Charter. At no time during the early days of American involvement in the Dominican Republic did the President directly seek full congressional approval.

This unilateral armed intervention continued until it was supplemented by a multilateral force of the Organization of American States, organized as a result of an OAS resolution requesting governments of member states who were willing to do so to make available to the OAS contingents of their land, naval, air, or police forces to form an Inter-American Peace Force which was to operate under the authority of the organization.[34] Following this resolution certain United States armed contingents were withdrawn from the Dominican Republic, and the remainder were incorporated into the Peace Force under a unified command.

Finally, there was the American involvement in Vietnam, an involvement which began following the termination of hostilities between the French army and the Viet Minh in 1954. Its time of commencement is usually calculated as being during the Eisenhower administration, although it should be noted that even before the ending of the conflict between the French and the Viet Minh, President Truman had sent some thirty-five military advisers to the country. By the end of President Eisenhower's administration, this number had increased to about one hundred. Increased participation was ordered by President Kennedy. At the time of his death some sixteen to seventeen thousand troops had been sent to Vietnam, and a rapid buildup was under way. Aerial combat operations began under the Kennedy administration, when American crews began to fly armed helicopters. The Kennedy administration viewed United States military involvement as necessary to prevent the collapse of South Vietnam and further to prevent the domino theory from becoming a reality—that is, to prevent the fall of all states of southeast Asia to communism one by one.[35]

President Johnson augmented the American military presence to vast proportions, so that South Vietnam could be aided to win "its contest against the externally directed and supported Communist conspiracy."[36] This American commitment was to become one of the costliest military ventures in both men and treasure ever conducted by the United States. It was exceeded only by the Civil War and the two World Wars in deaths in combat; and in the expenditure of money it exceeded all but World War II. It lasted longer than any other war in the history of the United States. Such a large commitment of troops to combat abroad should, it would seem, have called for a declaration of war by the Congress, but none was forthcoming and none was desired by the administration. Indeed, Undersecretary of State Katzenbach stated a belief that since war had been outlawed and since armed force could not be used under the United Nations Charter except in an exercise of a right of self-defense or pursuant to collective United Nations action, a declaration of war as such had lost its international significance.[37]

Furthermore, President Johnson assumed that following post–World War II precedent and practice, there was no need for Congress to "authorize the use of troops abroad if their use was to be constitutional."[38] On the contrary, he felt that while any formal support from Congress was welcome, the independent power of the executive was sufficient. Not until the Gulf of Tonkin Resolution of August 10, 1964, was there specific congressional "approval" of U.S. involvement in Southeast Asia. This resolution, which passed the House of Representatives unanimously and the Senate with only two dissenting votes, stated that

the Congress approves and supports the determination of the President, as Commander-in-Chief, to take all necessary measures to repel any armed attack against the forces of the United States and to prevent further aggression . . . consonant with the Constitution of the United States . . . the United States is therefore prepared, as the President determines, to take the necessary steps, including the use of armed force, to assist any member or protocol state [of the SEATO] requesting assistance in defense of its freedom.[39]

Approving and supporting the acts of the President to repel armed attacks against the U.S. forces would seem merely to reaffirm the original Constitutional Convention agreement that a President can repel an armed attack against the nation or its forces in accordance with his own powers. The second part of the resolution permitting action "as the President determines" and authorizing "all necessary steps" seems to banish any idea of the ability of Congress to limit the presidential use of military force abroad. And it was so interpreted, for in congressional testimony in 1967 it was formally asserted on behalf of an administration spokesman that the resolution together with the SEATO Treaty consti-

tuted a "functional declaration of war," thus combining the resolution
with a treaty to assert modification of the explicit congressional power
to declare war.[40]

In other words, while Congress has the power to declare war, this
power does not mandate a formal declaration whenever Congress intends to authorize the conduct of war by the President. The immediate
furor which caused the congressional approval resolution was an alleged
attack on United States naval units off the coast of North Vietnam.
Actually, however, the resolution had been drafted and prepared some
time before the naval incident and had been brought forth by the administration at the proper emotional time for congressional passage.[41]

The resolution did grant a broad authority to the President, but at
least in the mind of President Johnson it was not needed. To him the
presidential prerogative was sufficient to support the presidential action
in the conflict in Vietnam.[42]

Nevertheless, other legal justifications for the presidential action in
Vietnam have been asserted. The SEATO Treaty[43] has been referred to.
It recognizes that an armed attack against a member state would endanger the peace and security of all members, so that each should act
to meet the common danger in accord with constitutional processes. It
further provides that if the territory, sovereignty, or political independence of any party is threatened in ways other than by armed attack, the
parties shall consult in order to agree upon measures which should be
taken for the common defense. Any such action was to be taken only
with the consent of the state whose territory has been subjected to the
aggression. The parties to the treaty designated Laos, Cambodia, and
South Vietnam as nonsignatories to which the treaty extended.

Since the treaty speaks of meeting the common danger in accord
with the constitutional processes of each country, we are, therefore, faced
by this statement with the question: just what are the constitutional
processes in the United States with regard to a constitutional use of
armed force? Undersecretary of State Katzenbach attempted to justify
armed action in Vietnam by pointing out that SEATO and the Tonkin
Resolution were in fact the "functional equivalent" of a declaration of
war by the Congress.[44]

An even more expansive theory has been presented by the legal
adviser to the State Department. His theory is based upon the fact that
the President has the right to use armed force defensively, and that the
commitment extends to individual and collective self-defense which is

recognized by the United Nations Charter. Under that instrument armed force is for the most part forbidden except to meet an armed attack, through the exercise of an independent or collective right of self-defense. Thus when South Vietnam is attacked, that country has a right of self-defense, and the United States is entitled by international law to assist in repelling that attack under its inherent right of collective self-defense. The power of the President envisaged by the framers to repel sudden attacks upon the United States has grown so that an attack on another nation vital to the security of the United States is considered an attack upon the United States.[45]

Critics of the United States involvement disputed these contentions, claiming among other things not only that there had been no armed attack on South Vietnam to justify a right of self-defense under the UN Charter, but that the conflict in South Vietnam was in reality a civil war into which other nations were not authorized to intervene militarily by the United Nations or by international law.[46]

Nevertheless, when President Johnson made his decision to continue to send a large number of troops into Southeast Asia in the spring of 1965, he sought and obtained another vote from Congress through an appropriations bill accompanied by a message which read:

This is not a routine appropriation. For each member of Congress who supports this request is also voting to persist in our effort to halt Communist aggression in South Vietnam. Each is saying that the Congress and the President stand united before the world in joint determination that the independence of South Vietnam shall be preserved and the Communist attack will not succeed.[47]

The committee reports and debates associated with this appropriation made it clear that the vote was indeed a reaffirmation of the Gulf of Tonkin Resolution policy and its implementation. Comparable debates and votes occurred in 1966 as well.[48]

President Nixon pledged to withdraw American troops from South Vietnam, and in 1973 the Paris Agreement on Ending the War and Restoring Peace in Vietnam was signed so that withdrawal was to become a reality.[49] Nevertheless, in the interim period and prior to the Paris Agreement, the Nixon government enlarged the conflict. In 1970, the much-criticized invasion of neutral Cambodia was launched on the ground that the buildup of North Vietnamese troops in sanctuaries in that country threatened the safety of the American armed forces. Nixon

based his action constitutionally upon his power as Commander-in-Chief
and the defense and protection of the American military. He stated:
"I shall meet my responsibility as Commander-in-Chief to take the
action I consider necessary to defend the security of our American men."[50]
Later air incursions over North Vietnam and Laos, as well as Cambodia,
were ordered, and in 1972 the mining of Haiphong Harbor was ordered
by the President.[51]

In 1971, burning disagreement in the Congress with the Vietnam war
caused the repeal by that body of the Tonkin Gulf Resolution.[52] The
Nixon administration had, however, largely disowned the resolution
prior to the repeal and had placed legal reliance upon presidential constitutional power alone, primarily the Commander-in-Chief power.[53]
Congress also, in an attempt to end enlargement of the war, had seen
fit to cut off funds for various operations in the area.[54] In 1973 and over
a presidential veto the Congress enacted the War Powers Resolution
which sought to clarify the question of presidential powers vis-à-vis
congressional powers in the initiation of armed hostilities.[55] This document requires close presidential consultation with the Congress when
United States armed forces are to be introduced into a foreign country
in a situation other than when there has been a declaration of war.
Constitutional and interpretational problems are raised by this resolution.

It should be noted that up to now the document has seemingly
been of little hindrance to the unilateral exercise of presidential power.
In 1975 President Ford was faced with the problem of the evacuation
of Americans, members of the armed forces and civilians who remained
in South Vietnam, as well as certain Vietnamese, from the military over-
run of South Vietnam and the debacle which confronted that country.
A request for clarification of presidential power under the War Powers
Resolution was pending when action for evacuation became immediately
necessary.[56] The President ordered troops to effectuate the evacuation on
his own authority. Although it was generally believed that the President
had authority to evacuate American citizens, there was disagreement as
to his powers to act for foreign nationals. The executive department
maintained that its actions were justified on grounds of moral authority.[57]

A very short time later, military force was used to rescue the American merchant ship *Mayaguez* and her crew. The President did not consult the Congress as the War Powers Resolution demanded, but notified
them after he took the action. Moreover, he explained that his action
rested upon a constitutional basis of the Commander-in-Chief power.[58]

5

PRESIDENTIAL ACKNOWLEDGMENTS OF EXCLUSIVE CONGRESSIONAL POWER

WHEN CONSIDERATION IS GIVEN to the number of incidents and military actions conducted abroad by executive authority without congressional authorization and the assertions we have noted of presidential power to conduct them in this manner, one cannot but become impressed with a supposition that through words and practice presidential prerogative may well have become standard constitutional operating procedure. At this point, then, it behooves us to stop and take stock of certain presidential voices expressive of a different view. From the statements of these Presidents as well as their hesitancies or refusals to resort to armed force in the absence of congressional authorization or declaration, we can infer a belief that the war-making power does rest exclusively in the Congress with the possible exception of defensive military action.[1]

Allusion is often made to the pronouncement of Thomas Jefferson to the Congress when in 1801 a defensive naval force was ordered to Tripoli in the face of a declaration of war by Tripoli against the United States. Jefferson announced that the President could order only defensive action in the absence of a congressional sanction. Some ambiguity exists as to Jefferson's true beliefs, in the light of orders given to the commander of the naval squadron prior to its departure from the United States which would authorize offensive action, and this without congressional authorization. Perhaps his modest expression of presidential power to the Congress was a political tactic to induce the Congress to authorize offensive measures—which the Congress saw fit to do.[2]

A more clear-cut assertion of conviction that congressional power to declare war restricts presidential uses of force is Jefferson's statement in 1805, prompted by Spanish intrusions into territory claimed by the United States as part of the Louisiana purchase. Jefferson affirmed that only Congress was empowered to change the condition of peace to the condition of war and admitted that he was duty bound to await congressional authority for a resort to force.[3]

President Madison used words of a similar tenor in 1812 when reporting certain British outrages upon United States commerce. After noting that protests had failed to stop the outrages, he declared that the Constitution had wisely confided to the legislative department the issue as to "[w]hether the United States shall continue passive under these progressive usurpations and these accumulating wrongs, or, opposing force to force in defense of their national rights commit a just cause into the hands of the Almighty Disposer of events. . . ."[4] It should be remembered that President Madison was most reluctant to become embroiled in the War of 1812, no matter who authorized the resort to military means. Firebrands in the Congress, not the President, brought on that body's declaration of war.[5]

In 1824 President Monroe was called upon by Colombia to enforce his own doctrine to prevent threats of aggression by France against Colombia. Specifically, France had demanded the imposition of a Colombian monarch as a condition of French recognition of Colombia's independent nationhood. Monroe commented to Madison that the "Executive has no right to compromit the nation in any question of war . . . ," and replied to Colombia that the "ultimate decision of the question belongs to the Legislative Department of Government."[6] One has a feeling that President Monroe welcomed a way out and an opportunity to pass the buck to the Congress. The United States was too weak in those days to enforce the Monroe Doctrine. During the early history of the Republic, the job of enforcement of the doctrine's provisions, to the extent that they were enforced, fell to the British Navy.

President Andrew Jackson, who normally was far from timid in advancing presidential power, displayed unusual restraint by recognizing the exclusive war-making power of the Congress. In the case of Texas, he even refrained from exercising the constitutional power of recognition of a new nation or its government. He reasoned that such recognition would probably lead to war with Mexico. Therefore, it behooved the President to reach an understanding even as to recognition with the body which alone could declare war.[7]

Daniel Webster, speaking as secretary of state for President Fillmore, expressed a similar viewpoint but more bluntly when, in speaking of a threatened French attack on Hawaii, he stated that "the war making power rests entirely with Congress."[8]

The United States under President Buchanan refused to join in an Anglo-French expedition against Peking in 1857. The ground for the United States refusal was that military expeditions demanded congressional authority, since the war-making power was vested in Congress.[9] On several other occasions Buchanan requested congressional authorization for a use of armed force, stating that the President "cannot legitimately resort to force without the direct authority of Congress except in resisting and repelling attacks."[10]

As noted earlier, Abraham Lincoln abjured unauthorized presidential uses of force when he was a congressman; but when President he ordered belligerent action against the Confederacy without congressional approval. That action was later ratified by Congress.[11]

In 1869, Haiti attacked the Dominican Republic. As a result President Grant authorized the use of naval force against Haiti. Senate disapproval caused a withdrawal of the presidential order. On a later occasion, when violations of American rights occurred in Cuba, he communicated to the Congress that he would at a future time recommend that which would be necessary to cope with the situation.[12]

When a problem of lawlessness on the Mexican border arose during the administration of President Arthur, he called the matter to congressional attention and spoke of a possible need for congressional legislation to suppress the lawlessness. Later, when Arthur was confronted with difficulties arising from the fact that the War of the Pacific was being fought by Peru and Bolivia on one side and Chile on the other, he did not attempt armed intervention to dictate the peace, either alone or through the Congress. He did, however, report the facts to Congress.[13]

In a message to Congress in 1891, President Harrison reported difficulties with Chile which arose from an attack upon United States sailors in Valparaiso. Congress was informed that if Chile did not respond satisfactorily to a note forwarded by the government of the United States to that of Chile, the President would ask Congress to take the necessary action. Chile paid the indemnity, thus settling the matter.[14]

One author has pointed to the fact that Presidents Wilson and Franklin D. Roosevelt, although resorting to unneutral acts against Germany prior to World Wars I and II which might have helped to draw this country into the wars, did not actually commit the nation to combat on foreign soil without a congressional declaration of war.[15] Such reticence by these two Presidents at this point in history could hardly demonstrate a belief that they, as President, had no constitutional power in all situations to resort to a use of force on their own. Indeed, President Wilson had little compunction in ordering a military occupation of Haiti and the Dominican Republic without congressional authorization. The same can be said as to General Pershing's incursions into Mexico in hot pursuit of Pancho Villa.[16]

President Roosevelt with his Good Neighbor Policy sought to abandon the use of force in foreign policy, particularly in Latin America, whether authorized by Congress or not. With his great sense of the political he surely knew that war with the Axis Powers was unpopular with the Congress until the United States was attacked at Pearl Harbor, and that an unauthorized used of force by the President prior to that attack would have tended to tear the nation apart.[17] After the attack and the declarations of war upon this country by the Axis, Congress gave its assent with near unanimity.

It is not easy to pass judgment upon the credit which should be extended to these presidential admissions of exclusive or near exclusive power of Congress to make war which demonstrate a recognition of severe limits on presidential power to commit troops to combat without legislative authority. Did cognizance of the constitutional war-declaring power of Congress actually deter these Presidents from uses of force abroad which they would otherwise have ordered in what they believed to be the best interests of the nation? Corwin would seem to negate such a notion in a belief that such statements are largely words, words, words. He calls such presidential words of deference "gestures of obeisance to Congress's 'power to declare war.' "[18] Certainly it would appear to be true that in many instances, ranging from Jefferson's disclaimers of presidential war to Roosevelt's careful statement explaining in his message of sympathy to France in 1940 that only the Congress can make military commitments, such presidential expressions were motivated by a political posturing which at the time was the better part of valor. On some occasions a glance at history gives one a feeling that the deferential attitudes of Presidents to the Congress may have resulted from the fact that the President did not desire to use force anyway and excused himself on the ground that he had no power to do so. Moreover, some Presidents seem to have changed their minds over the issue. Grant became cautious as to presidential power and deferential to congressional power only after he had been slapped by the Senate in the Haitian–Dominican Republic affair. And Lincoln disavowed all thought of presidential power prior to his presidency but resorted to force with little deference to the Congress when he became President.

Nevertheless, and even though the presidential statements may be expressive of lip service to the Congress or at times self-serving, they still are indications of historical precedent for the position that the constitutional norm negates a principle of presidential prerogative to make war. Of course, examples of the use of force by the President without congressional authorization or declaration also abound. But in any event there are historical precedents and practices which recognize limits upon presidential power in favor of Congress.

6

CONSTITUTIONAL AND INTERNATIONAL, LAW BASES

POWER TO DECLARE WAR

THE CONSTITUTION OF THE UNITED STATES grants to the Congress with precision and with clarity the power to declare war.[1] Thus it seems somewhat anomalous that from the beginning of the nation's history presidential power to use armed force against a foreign nation or nations has been exercised with no such declaration or indeed without congressional authorization of any kind.[2] Since the belief is prevalent that the founding fathers intended the power to declare war was to be an exclusive legislative power not to be shared by the executive, and since war is a contention between states through the use of their armed forces, it becomes necessary to determine what the founding fathers intended to include under the rubric "to declare war."

A declaration of war is simply a communication made by one nation state to another that the status of peace which has existed between them is now terminated and a status of war has taken its place.[3] Thus the congressional power to declare war could be understood to mean merely the power to make the formal declaration or communication.

36

As such the power would be a limited one. Congress would be assigned a very minor role in the decisional process as to the use of armed force by the United States, if this is all that is signified. Inasmuch as it has long been recognized that hostilities between and among nation states can exist without a declaration of war, such a restrictive interpretation could be regarded as tantamount to enabling the President to engage in all sorts of undeclared warlike hostilities. He would then be the real initiator, leaving to Congress only the authority of making the declaration. Actually, the formal declaration of war has fallen into disuse. In 1961 Undersecretary of State Katzenbach stated that it was outmoded.[4] Historically there have been few cases of formal declarations of war. The United States has engaged in a number of armed hostilities with foreign nations since becoming a nation,[5] but only five formal declarations of war have been made, and in four of these war existed before the declaration.[6]

It is extremely doubtful that the framers of the Constitution intended such a limited assignment to the Congress, and it is generally agreed that the power to commit the United States to war, the power to initiate war, was intended to be vested in the Congress alone, insofar as the determination was to be made by the United States and not by the foreign enemy. Alexander Hamilton, in a statement uttered not too many years after the framing of the Constitution, adopted such a viewpoint. He said:

"The Congress shall have the power to declare war"; the plain meaning of which is, that it is the peculiar and exclusive duty of Congress, *when the nation is at peace*, to change that state into a state of war; whether from calculations of policy, or from provocations or injuries received; in other words, it belongs to Congress only to go to war. But when a foreign nation declares or openly and avowedly makes war upon the United States, they are then by the very fact *already at war*, and any declaration on the part of Congress is nugatory: it is at least unnecessary.[7]

This is further borne out by the debates at the Constitutional Convention. The first draft of the new charter would have given the Congress the power "to make" war.[8] The framers thus sought to limit presidential or executive authority because they feared to grant to a single individual the power to commit the nation to the dreadful consequences of war. They had witnessed a hard and bitter war for which blame was placed upon the British king, an executive empowered to initiate war. In the light of this experience they sought to clip the executive's wings by placing the power to initiate war, declared or undeclared, in the whole Congress, subject to approval or veto by the President. Justice Story stated the reasonings of the founding fathers well in the following words:

> . . . the power of declaring war is not only the highest sovereign prerogative, but that it is in its own nature and effects so critical and calamitous, that it requires the utmost deliberation, and the successive review of all councils of the nation. War, in its best estate, never fails to impose upon the people the most burthesome taxes, and personal sufferings. It is always injurious to, and sometimes subversive to the great commercial, manufacturing, and agricultural interests. Nay, it always involves the prosperity, and not unfrequently the existence, of a nation. It is sometimes fatal to public liberty itself, by introducing a spirit of military glory, which is ready to follow, wherever a successful commander will lead; and in a republic, whose institutions are essentially founded on the basis of peace, there is infinite danger, that war will find it both imbecile in defence, and eager for contest. Indeed, the history of republics has but too fatally proved, that they are too ambitious of military frame and conquest, and too easily devoted to the views of demagogues, who flatter their pride and betray their interests. It should therefore be difficult in a republic to declare war, but not to make peace. The representatives of the people are to lay the taxes to support a war, and therefore should be consulted, as to its time, and the ways and means of making it effective. The co-operation of all the branches of the legislative power ought, upon principle, to be required in this the highest act of legislation, as it is in all others. Indeed, there might be a propriety even in enforcing still greater restrictions, as by requiring a concurrence of two thirds of both houses.[9]

But what is war? Not all instances of armed conflict between nations have been considered to be war either under the principles of constitutional law or under international law. For example, according to some authorities "war is a state or condition of affairs, not simply successive acts of force. . . ." Further, a legal state of war may exist without the conduct of hostilities, just as hostilities may be conducted in the absence of a legal state of war.[10] If armed force may be used by one state against another and not constitute war, it would follow that armed conflict other than war would fall without the exclusive congressional power which pertains to a declaration of war only. Thus, how is war to be defined for which congressional declaration and initiation should be required?

Vattel, in an oft-quoted definition, describes war as ". . . that state in which we prosecute our rights by force."[11] Westlake states that "war is the state or condition of governments contending by force." Justice Bushrod Washington in an early Supreme Court case, *Bas v. Tingy*,[12] regards war as "contention between two nations in external matters under the authority of their respective governments. . . ."[13] Oppenheim adds something more to the definition that is a use of force between states or governments. He would define war as "a contention between two or more States through their armed forces, for the purpose of overpowering each other and imposing such conditions of peace as the victor pleases."[14]

If war is defined solely in a material sense as a use of force, as the existence of hostilities, then it would seem that all hostilities or at least those of some magnitude between states or governments would be war, and yet it has been admitted that not all international uses of armed force give rise to a state of war. More has traditionally been required for armed hostilities to be considered as war in the international legal sense. The additional requisite is intent, an intent to make war, an *animus belligerendi*. As Quincy Wright has stated:

War in the legal sense means a period of time during which the extraordinary laws of war and neutrality have superseded the normal law of peace in the relations of states. . . . It appears that any state has power to convert a state of peace into a state of war by an overt act manifesting its intention to do so.[15]

Stone points out:

International war is a relation of two or more governments to at least one other government in which at least one of such governments no longer permits its relation with the other or others to be governed by the laws of peace.[16]

To the contrary, the laws of peace give way to international laws and rules pertaining to war concerning permissible methods of war, limits of violence which may be resorted to between the parties, and the nonobservance or abrogation of certain treaties which have existed between the contenders, as well as concerning rules governing the neutrality of third states. Thus war comes about when one nation intends such a state of war to exist governed by the special law or laws pertaining to

war, not peace. This intention may be manifested by a declaration of
war or by a formal ultimatum to the other party. In the absence of
such a formal declaration or ultimatum, proof may be found in informal
statements by the initiating contender that it is seeking a total military
defeat of the other, or by the attacked state that it considers the use of
force against it as constituting a state of war. Moreover, in the absence
of clear-cut declarations, formal or informal, the intent may be found
by the nature of the acts of hostility themselves which each of the
contending parties commits against the other. Evidence of the legal
intent may be found through the extent of military operations and
preparations, for example whether a general mobilization is called for.
A call for the observance of neutrality by third states would indicate the
existence of a state of war, as would the establishment of blockade, or
the rupture of diplomatic and consular relations.[17]

A state of war then can be said to be in being when a nation
especially so declares; where without express declaration it uses force
against another state and accompanies such use by indicators from which
the *animus belligerendi* can be deduced; and finally where a state
utilizes force against another without the legal intent of war, but the
state against which the force is used determines to treat such acts as acts
creating a state of war. On the other hand, even though the hostilities
between the parties may be serious and long-continued, the viewpoint
prevails among many authorities that war does not occur if the contenders disclaim a state of war as existing between them and refuse to
admit an *animus belligerendi*, unless perhaps third parties from the acts
of the contenders may recognize a state of war as existent through the
issuance of a proclamation of neutrality.

Wright, for example, has said:

Suppose, however, that a state commits acts of war on a large scale, but
with repeated assertions that it is not intending to make war, is it possible
for its acts to speak louder than its words? It is believed that such a situation may become a state of war, but only if recognized as such by the victim
or by third parties.[18]

The state of war doctrine, also called *de jure* war, war in the legal
sense, or war in the international legal sense, which is dependent upon
the subjective element of intent of the parties to make war, has been
the subject of dispute as among jurists. Many refuse to regard war as a
status, but look upon it as an action, that is, that it is brought about

by acts of war, the use of armed force. The *animus belligerendi* is played down. War in the material sense is regarded as giving rise to war in the legal sense.[19] The difficulty here is that not all acts of force are regarded as war, and although war in the material sense is often alluded to by courts and governmental proclamations, still such material acts of war are to be distinguished from war in the legal sense. Thus some jurists have sought to retain in the concept of war the *animus belligerendi* and also include, at least in certain situations, the concept of war in the material sense. As to the latter, the acts of force cannot be considered as war unless they are of large dimensions. Localized or limited acts of force will not do. Brierly states the viewpoint well:

If acts of force are sufficiently serious and long-continued, then, even if both sides disclaim any *animus belligerendi* and refuse to admit that a state of war has arisen between them then there comes a point at which law must say to the parties "you are refusing to recognize the facts; your actions are of the kind which it is the policy of international law to characterize as 'war'; and therefore, whatever you choose to say about it, you have in fact set up a state of things which in the eye of the law is a state of war."[20]

War may also be conceived of as war in the legal sense and war in the material sense, both of which may be regarded as a legal situation at international law. As one jurist has pointed out, the legal state of war, which he calls formal war, is that which requires the intent to wage war.[21] Material war is conceived to be hostilities carried on for some length of time and of some extended dimensions. The principal difference between the two has to do with the legal consequences arising from the two types of war. Formal war carries with it all the laws of war and neutrality of international law. Material war, on the other hand, only brings into being certain of these rules. A selective application of the rules is to be made to the extent necessary. For example, the rules of war which relate to the material conduct of war are necessarily applicable in a material war.[22]

Recognizing the conflicting viewpoints as to the concept and meaning of war on the international level, what can be said concerning the meaning for purposes of the United States Constitution? Can we conclude that the constitutional law meaning of war as perhaps intended by the founding fathers is synomymous with war in the formal or international law sense only, or does it include war in the material sense? Unless the constitutional concept includes the latter also, then a declaration of war by the Congress would be requisite only when there was intent on the part of the United States to wage war. Acts of force of long duration and of magnitude would probably not necessitate such a congressional declaration, and certainly limited acts of violence conducted against another government would not.

The framers of the Constitution must have known of the meaning of war in the legal sense, for the classical writers from Grotius onward had come to describe war as a legal status.[23] Thus it can be reasoned that the congressional declaration of war was definitely required in order to bring about a constitutional initiation of a legal or formal state of war as known at international law. But how about material war?

The courts of the United States have recognized the distinction between war in the legal sense and war in the material sense, although they have not always used those words. In *Bas v. Tingy*, the Supreme Court of the United States recognized statuses known as solemn war and imperfect or limited war. In this case there was involved an American ship which had been captured by a French privateer in 1799, recaptured by a public armed American ship, and condemned to pay salvage under an Act of Congress. Upon appeal to the Supreme Court of the United States, it was held that at the time of the capture and recapture limited hostilities existed between France and the United States which had been authorized by the two governments and which justified the legislation in question. The United States authorization had come from the Congress, although not in the form of a declaration of war.

Justice Bushrod Washington stated in his opinion:

It may, I believe, be safely laid down, that every contention by force between two nations, in external matters, under the authority of their respective governments, is not only war, but public war. If it be declared in form, it is called solemn, and is of the perfect kind; because one whole nation is at war with another whole nation; and all the members of the nation declaring war, are authorized to commit hostilities against all the members of the other, in every place and under every circumstance. In such a war all the members act under a general authority, and all the rights and consequences of war attach to their condition.

But hostilities may subsist between two nations more confined in its nature and extent; being limited as to places, persons, and things; and this is more properly termed imperfect war; because not solemn, and because those who are authorized to commit hostilities, act under special authority, and can go no further than to the extent of their commission. Still, however, it is a public war, because it is an external contention by force between some members of the two nations, authorized by the legitimate powers. It is a war between two nations though all the members are not authorized to commit hostilities such as in a solemn war, where the government restrains the general power.[24]

This latter was the condition which the court declared to have existed between France and the United States in 1799.

In this same case, Justice Chase, in his opinion, stated:

Congress is empowered to declare a general war, or Congress may wage a limited war in place, in objects, and in time. If a general war is declared its extent and operations are only restricted and regulated by the *jus belli*, forming a part of the laws of nations; but if a partial war is waged, its extent and operation depend on our municipal laws.

What then is the nature of the contest subsisting between America and France? In my judgment it is a limited, partial, war. Congress has not declared war in general terms; but Congress has authorized hostilities on the high seas by certain persons in certain cases.[25]

Although the terms limited, partial, imperfect war have been designated as "mere words with no legal meaning behind them," is it possible to compare these terms to what has been described as material war and to speak of the perfect or solemn war as synonomous with war in the legal or international legal sense? The latter interpretation is obviously true, but it would seem that the imperfect or limited or partial war is, in the minds of the justices, war in the legal sense also, inasmuch as the Congress by its legislation is deemed to have intended a state of war with France, although a limited or partial one. Moreover, material war as discussed above would not necessarily be confined to a limited use of force.

Bas v. Tingy does say that limited or partial war is also war. Thus if it is war, then one can conclude that Congress must initiate it either by its own authorization, which of course was done in this instance of American-French hostilities, or by specific declaration.

Is the imperfect, limited war situation—a situation short of general war—subject to the exclusive initiation by Congress? It has been contended that it is, and that great weight should be given to the opinions in *Bas v. Tingy* because they are interpretations by contemporaries of the framers and as such are persuasive as to the framers' meanings and intentions. Nevertheless, another contemporaneous opinion sheds doubt.

Chief Justice Marshall in *Little v. Barreme*,[26] a case also arising from the French-American hostilities, had before him presidential instructions which collided with congressional instructions. President Adams had instructed the United States Navy to seize American vessels bound to or from French ports. Congress had authorized such seizure only when such vessels were bound to or sailing to French territory. Chief Justice Marshall recognized that the congressional authorization must control, and in a previous case he had accepted the general-war-partial-war theories of *Bas v. Tingy*. But in *Little v. Barreme* he also said:

It is by no means clear that the President of the United States whose high duty it is to "take care that the laws be faithfully executed," and who is commander in chief of the armies and navies of the United States, might not, without any special authority for that purpose, in the then existing state of things, have empowered the officers commanding the armed vessels of the United States, to seize and send into port for adjudication, American vessels which were forfeited by being engaged in illicit commerce. But when it is observed . . . that the 5th section [of the act of Congress] gives a special authority to seize on the high seas and limits that authority to the seizure of vessels bound or sailing to a French port, the legislature seems to have prescribed that the manner in which this law shall be carried into execution, was to exclude a seizure of any vessel not bound to a French port.[27]

It will be noted that Chief Justice Marshall, though not certain, does not completely preclude the use of armed force by the President in this partial war situation without congressional authority. Although he speaks to the effect that the armed force might be directed by the President against an American vessel, could the force also have been directed against the foreign power—for example, French ships—in the pursuance of his powers faithfully to execute the laws and as Commander-in-Chief? If this be true, then Congress is not given the exclusive power to initiate war, for the President would also share the power with respect to partial or imperfect war or war in the material sense, which would not be considered as war for purposes of the Constitution. In other words, it could be said that the constitutional use of the word *war* refers to war in the international legal sense.

This would seem to be further borne out by Justice Nelson's opinion in the *Prize Cases*.[28] These had to do with the constitutional question of President Lincoln's power to initiate the Civil War specifically through a proclamation and enforcement of a naval blockade without a declaration of war by the Congress. The majority sustained the President's action on the ground that he was constitutionally empowered to recognize hostile acts of rebels or of a foreign nation as initiating a state of war in the legal sense and that he need not await a congressional declaration. Justice Nelson, writing the opinion for the four dissenters in the case, believed that a blockade could be legally established only when a state of public war existed and that such public war could be commenced only by the Congress. As to what constituted war, Justice Nelson went on to say:

An idea seems to be entertained that all that was necessary to constitute war was organized hostility, conflicts on land and on sea—the taking of towns and capture of fleets—in fine, the magnitude and dimensions of the resistance against the Government—constituted war with all the belligerent rights belonging to civil war. . . .

Now in one sense, no doubt this is war, and may be a war of the most extensive and threatening dimensions and effects, but it is a state simply of its existence in a material sense, and has no relevancy or weight when the question is, what constitutes war in a legal sense, or in the sense of the law of nations, and of the Constitution of the United States? For it must be a war in this sense to attach to it all the consequences that belong to belligerent rights. Instead, therefore, of inquiring after armies and navies, and victories lost and won, or organized rebellion against the General Government, the inquiry should be into the law of nations and into the municipal fundamental laws of the Government. For we find there that to constitute a civil war in the sense in which we are speaking, before it can exist, in contemplation of law, it must be recognized or declared by the sovereign power of the state.[29]

This language clearly indicates that the term *war* as used in the Constitution is to be equated with war in the international legal sense. War, then, in the United States is that which has been declared by the Congress. It is a legal state or condition, and in the words of Justice Nelson, war in the material sense has no relevance as to "what constitutes war in a legal sense." Following this line of thought it would seem that armed force, at least as justified by the law of nations, could be constitutionally carried on in the absence of congressional declaration as long as there was no intent to wage war in the legal sense.

It should be noted that Justice Nelson was of the opinion that the blockade as an act of war was illegal at international law without war in the legal sense. Such argument can perhaps be made as to a blockade between belligerents in time of war. But international law has also recognized pacific blockade, a blockade instituted in time of peace.[30] This could be said to constitute war in a material sense but not in the legal sense, and as such would appear to be constitutionally permissible without congressional authorization.

Although Justice Nelson's was a dissenting opinion, the distinction between war in the legal sense and in the material sense which he recognized was not denied by the majority. And at a later period, at the end of the nineteenth century and the beginning of the twentieth, a series of decisions incorporating a similar theory were rendered by the Court of Claims. Like *Bas v. Tingy*, these cases were concerned with the French-American hostilities of 1798-1801.[31] They arose out of an Act of Congress of 1885 by which the United States government assumed responsibility for losses by United States citizens which had occurred during the course of the hostilities.[32] The United States government was pressured to assume responsibility for these losses, inasmuch as it had waived spoilation claims in its settlement with the French government.[33] The attorney general of the United States argued before the Court of Claims that since there had been war with France, the United States had no claim against France in relation to captures in time of war; therefore no claims could be made against the United States government. The court in *Gray, Administrator v. United States*[34] disagreed, holding no war existed, thus disagreeing also with the decision in *Bas v. Tingy* which had termed the hostilities public war of an imperfect nature. After referring to the character of congressional legislation existing at the time of the hostilities, the court said:

This legislation shows that war was imminent; that protection of our commerce was ordered, but distinctly shows that in the opinion of the legislature, war did not in fact exist. . . . We are, therefore, of the opinion that no such war existed as operated to abrogate treaties, to suspend private rights, or to authorize indiscriminate seizures and condemnations; that in short there was no public general war but limited war in its nature similar to a prolonged series of reprisals.[35]

In other such spoilant claims cases the court again disagreed with the conclusion in *Bas v. Tingy* which had declared the hostilities to be public war. The Court of Claims in all these cases[36] appears to have adopted the notion that only a declaration by Congress could make the situation war, and even though certain hostilities were authorized by the Congress and even though force was actually resorted to, still war in the legal sense did not exist. Consequently that which is war must be intended by one of the parties, and this intent of war in the legal as distinguished from war in the material sense must in the United States be manifested by the Congress. Thus armed force amounting to material war could be carried on by the President if authorized by powers granted him by the Constitution. Congressional action would only become requisite to initiate a legal state of war, war in the legal sense, even though such acts might be of magnitude and of long duration.

Despite the fact that such a conclusion can be reached from the reasoning garnered from court opinions, objections have been taken to such a broad concept of presidential power. It has been contended that since the Constitution granted the war-declaring power to Congress in order to check presidential autocracy, the President should not be permitted to enter into any war declared or undeclared, with the possible exception of repelling a sudden attack, without the consent of Congress, and the nature of war, whether a state thereof or acts of force amounting to material war, is of no consequence.[37]

Others have looked at the admitted constitutional commitments to the President which make of him Commander-in-Chief in time of peace and in time of war, at his power over foreign relations, at his power faithfully to execute the law, including international law and the sanctioning of breaches of that law, as well as at the fact that only he can act with speed, secrecy, and authority, and have pointed out that he is constitutionally endowed to initiate unilaterally a use of force abroad. This reasoning, combined with the fact that presidential uses of force short of war have been condoned both in practice and by courts, has indicated that the President must have some power to resort to what might be described as a use of force on his own authority.[38] The problem comes at where the line shall be drawn. Shall it be the broad line drawn above based upon the distinction between war in the legal sense and war in the material sense? Some would agree to this. Others would call for a narrow concept based upon a test of actual or probable magnitude of hostilities. One jurist has approached the problem as follows:

As a dividing line for presidential authority in the use of the military abroad, one test might be to require congressional authorization in all cases where regular combat units are committed to sustain hostilities. This test would be likely to include most situations resulting in substantial casualties and substantial commitment of resources. . . . The test has the virtue of responsiveness to precisely those situations historically creating the greatest concern over presidential authority but like all tests is somewhat frayed at the edges. In conflicts which gradually escalate, the dividing line for requiring congressional authorization might be initial commitment to combat of regular United States combat units as such.[39]

This author would then call for congressional authorization in the material as well as legal sense, but would permit certain limited use of force by the President in limited situations, even with combat troops. The difficulty with this thesis is the drawing of the line in situations as to war in a material sense and limited acts of force as well as the problem of prediction as to when and whether there will be an escalation of a limited use of force to a use of magnitude, although the thesis does recognize that congressional authorization would be needed when the initial commitment to combat of United States forces ensues. This seems to conflict with his statement that authorization is needed only when combat units are committed to sustained hostilities. What if combat troops are committed to sporadic hostilities?

Other writers have come up with somewhat differing ideas. They reject a single definition of or meaning to be ascribed to war for all legal relationships, because the meaning of the word they find changes when used in differing legal contexts. Thus war will assume one meaning in an international law sense, another in a constitutional law sense, and still another in some other sense.

In order to ascertain the meaning of the word in one context or another one must ascertain the purpose of its use in that context. As we have seen, the purpose of its use in the United States constitutional context is to check the autocracy of the executive in favor of the legislative body. The war-declaring power was purposefully given to this latter organ because that body more nearly represented the will of the public and thus more nearly reflected public or popular sentiment. It was then reasoned that such a purpose demands that the legislature should approve a use of force at least of a magnitude which would involve risk of the lives of the citizenry and a large expenditure of the nation's resources.

It was reasoned further that a use of force against a foreign sovereign has moral and legal connotations for the nation which also demand approval by the organ of government most representative of the nation's people, and thus for this purpose also the power was given to the Congress. As a result, the Constitution would require approval by the Congress based upon the extent of the hostilities—a quantitative analysis —and also the Constitution would require such approval based upon the purpose for which the force is used and would prohibit even an insignificant use of force without congressional approval if utilized for the wrong purpose—a qualitative analysis would perforce have to be made. If the force were used to force the sovereign will of a foreign nation to pursue a certain political, economic, or even ideological course, it could be resorted to only with the consent of Congress. On the other hand, if the force were used in a neutral manner, say to protect lives and property of American citizens, or to enforce international law, then theoretically it was thought that here the sovereign will of the foreign state would not be involved.[40]

It will be noted that all theories permit some use of force by the President without congressional declaration. They differ on the degree of force which might permit the unilateral use or on the purpose of the force. Since the President is conceded by all to have some power to use force without congressional authorization, perhaps the riddle can be solved by turning to a consideration of his powers under the Constitution and constitutional interpretation.

THE CHIEF EXECUTIVE

Article II, Section I of the Constitution of the United States declares that "[t]he executive power shall be vested in a President of the United States of America." Almost from the time of inception of the government of the United States under the Constitution there has been controversy as to the meaning of this language. Do the words constitute a grant of all the generic powers inherent in the executive branch, a delegation of all of the executive powers which government is capable of possessing, or do they merely create the office and confer a title upon the President?[41] If the former, a formidable power indeed is parceled out, for the executive power has been said to be the vaguest of all the powers of government. It has been defined as an indefinite or undefined residuum of power.[42] If all possible executive power is conferred, then it has been concluded that the President possesses the absolute prerogative claimed by the Stuart kings, that is a power to do all necessary for the public good without the prescription of law and sometimes even against the law.[43] Theodore Roosevelt stated the idea in a somewhat more limited fashion. To him the President could act in time of emergency as the needs of the nation required, even though there was no specific authorization for his action, unless such action was forbidden by the Constitution or the laws.[44]

If the words of Article II, Section 1 are not a broad grant of power, but are merely intended to create the office and title, the power would be limited to those express grants of power delegated to the President by the Constitution or those reasonably implied therein and necessary and proper to their exercise.[45] President Taft was a leading proponent of this position.[46] This circumscribed view seems not to have prevailed, at least if one can analyze the various conflicting and diverse opinions of the Supreme Court to find some common thread running through a majority of the justices' opinions in the case of *Youngstown Sheet and Tube Co. v. Sawyer*[47] (the Steel Seizure case). There, only two justices accepted what may be stated to be the limited Taft position. They based their position upon the separation of powers doctrine, which would forbid the President from encroaching upon the legislative power of Congress. To them the only manner in which adequate power could be balanced with meaningful responsibility was to restrict the President's power to those specifically granted to him by the Constitution and delegated to him by legislation. These two opinions would indicate that the President would be forbidden to *declare* and *initiate* war, for that would be an encroachment upon the legislative power of the Congress and an action not expressly delegated to him by the Constitution. Even under such a theory, however, the President would seemingly not be denied the power to use armed forces short of war if such action were based upon certain of his constitutionally delegated powers.

The opinions of the other justices in the *Youngstown* case are much less restrictive. None of the opinions accept the Stuart prerogative, which would permit the executive to contravene the laws of the legislature if the public good demands. The Theodore Roosevelt stewardship doctrine apparently comes through largely intact with some small limitation or restriction. The majority of the opinions in the case would recognize that the President can act in an emergency if the Constitution and the laws do not forbid (Roosevelt's notion). According to these opinions the executive would also be precluded from action if the policy of Congress which had not formally been reduced to law also forbade.

A theme runs through the concurring opinions, and to a degree in the dissenting opinion, which would recognize that an inherent presidential or executive power is available only in the case of a serious emergency and with the express or implied consent of the Congress. Following this theory, the President in the normal situation would possess only those powers specifically granted to him by the Constitution and the laws. Nevertheless he can exercise prerogative in an emergency with congressional acquiescence. Would this include the initiation of war in an emergency, even if self-defense of the nation were not invoked, so long as Congress acquiesces? Possibly. It must be stressed, however, that Congress must give its consent explicitly or implicitly, and even under this broad theory the President could not act in the absence of such congressional approbation. Therefore, reliance can hardly be placed upon inherent power of the chief executive if the *Youngstown* case is controlling. In order to find constitutional authority for a presidential use of armed force in the absence of congressional assent, we are thrown back to other constitutional principles or congeries of principles for sustenance. Constitutional bases for such presidential uses of force have been said to rest upon a theory of self-defense against attack, upon the President's constitutional power emanating from the fact that the constitution makes of him the Commander-in-Chief of the armed forces, from his foreign relations power, and from his duty to execute the laws faithfully.

THEORY OF SELF-DEFENSE

The first draft of the proposed Constitution as considered by the founding fathers granted to the Congress the power "[t]o make war." This language was changed upon the motion of Mr. Madison and Mr. Gerry. These gentlemen "moved to insert 'declare', striking out 'make' war; leaving to the Executive the power to repel sudden attacks."[48] Such a change was thought to be necessitated by the belief that the legislative body would by its very nature move too slowly to be vested with the power to act against a sudden attack. The motion was carried, and the change was effectuated. The Congress was given the power to declare war. As noted earlier, it is not generally thought that such change was intended to grant to the President the power to make war, in the sense of initiating war as distinguished from the conduct of the war after its initiation.[49] Nevertheless, the power of the President would extend to the taking of immediate defensive measures to repel a sudden attack against the nation; and although the framers of the Constitution by the language change can possibly be said to have intended such power to vest in the President, the power can also be said to be wider in scope and an inherent one growing from a right of national self-defense which would vest in the President the power to respond to such a sudden attack by the use of all military power, which he can muster as Commander-in-Chief of the armed forces.[50]

This conclusion has, however, been a subject of some controversy, especially as to the breadth of the power of the President to respond on his own even in the face of a declaration of war by another state, and one view of history proclaims that Jefferson was uncertain as to the extent of his power to act in self-defense.[51] In 1801, he sent a squadron of United States warships to the Mediterranean to protect United States commerce against threatened attack by Tripoli, one of the Barbary States. Prior to the arrival of the squadron, the Bey of Tripoli declared war. The commander of the squadron issued instructions to an officer who commanded a ship sailing to Malta for water to disarm and release vessels which might be captured on the way to Malta, but to seize vessels captured on the way back from Malta to Tripoli. A vessel captured on the journey to Malta was, in conformity with the instructions, released.

Thereafter Jefferson, in reporting to the Congress on the encounter, stated:

Unauthorized by the Constitution, without the sanction of Congress, to go beyond the line of defense, the vessel being disabled from committing further hostilities, was liberated with its crew. The Legislature will doubtless consider whether, by authorizing measures of offense also, they will place our force on an equal footing with that of its adversaries. I communicate all material information on this subject, that, in the exercise of this important function confided by the Constitution to the Legislature exclusively, their judgment may form itself on a knowledge and consideration of every circumstance of weight.[52]

Alexander Hamilton was highly critical of what appeared to be Jefferson's limited viewpoint on presidential power. He believed that when a state of war is thrust upon the United States by another country, the President can recognize the existence of a state of war and that no congressional declaration is needed for a waging of such war. He stated:

"The Congress shall have power to declare war"; the plain meaning of which is, that it is the peculiar and exclusive province of Congress, when the nation is at peace, to change that state into a state of war; whether from calculations of policy, or from provocations or injuries received; in other words, it belongs to Congress only *to go to war*. But when a foreign nation declares or openly and avowedly makes war upon the United States, they are then by the very fact *already at war*, and any declaration on the part of Congress is nugatory; it is at least unnecessary. . . .[53]

It would follow then that when a foreign nation attacks the United States with the intention to bring into existence a legal state of war, war exists and it behooves the President to accept the challenge as Commander-in-Chief and make war. The President does not initiate the war; the foreign nation initiates the war. Therefore a declaration of war by the Congress would be called for only when the United States initiates a war.

Actually the evidence would bear out the fact that Jefferson did not view presidential power in such a restrictive manner as Hamilton had come to believe in the face of Jefferson's statement to the Congress, for prior to the sailing of the squadron Jefferson had obtained instructions from the cabinet authorizing offensive action against states declaring war against the United States. Instructions according with these offensive instructions were issued to the commander of the squadron, who was authorized to sink, burn, capture, or destroy vessels attacking those of the United States. Therefore, Jefferson too in reality accepted a broad presidential war-making power, at least when confronted with a declaration of war by another state. The limited tenor of his language to the Congress was tactical to help persuade Congress to provide expressly for offensive action, which was indeed forthcoming. It did not indicate a belief that power to act offensively by the President was not constitutional.[54]

President Polk adhered to a position similar to that of Hamilton when he authorized military action against Mexico which resulted in the Battles of Palo Alto and Resaca de la Palma before Congress got around to a recognition of a state of war. He justified this action in a message to Congress in the following language:

After reiterated menaces, Mexico has passed the boundary of the United States, has invaded our territory and shed American blood upon the American soil. She has proclaimed that hostilities have commenced and that the two nations are now at war.

As war exists, and notwithstanding all our efforts to avoid it, exists by the act of Mexico herself, we are called upon by every consideration of duty and patriotism to vindicate with decision the honor, the rights and the interests of our country.

In further vindication of our rights and defense of our territory, I invoke the prompt action of Congress to recognize the existence of war, and to place at the disposition of the Executive the means of prosecuting the war with vigor, and thus hastening the restoration of peace.[55]

These interpretations of the President's power came from extrajudicial opinion. With the Supreme Court of the United States decision in *The Prize Cases*,[56] a judicial acceptance of the theories of Hamilton and Polk occurred. In *The Prize Cases* the Supreme Court held that the existence of war (the Civil War) may be recognized by the President in advance of congressional declaration, and that he may take action such as the establishment of a belligerent blockade which in time of peace he would not be constitutionally empowered to institute. Indeed the court seemingly recognizes a complete and unlimited power to defend and make war against a war begun through invasion by a foreign power or through rebellion. The court painted the picture in broad strokes:

By the Constitution, Congress alone has the power to declare a national or foreign war. . . . The Constitution confers on the President the whole executive power. He is bound to take care that the laws be faithfully executed. He is Commander-in-Chief of the [armed services and the militia of the several states when called into actual service]. He has no power to initiate or declare a war either against a foreign nation or domestic state. . . .

If a war be made by invasion of a foreign nation, the President is not only authorized but bound to resist force by force. He does not initiate the war, but is bound to accept the challenge without waiting for any special legislative authority. And whether the hostile party be a foreign invader, or States organized in rebellion, it is none the less a war, although the declaration of it be "unilateral."

This greatest of civil wars was not gradually developed by popular commotion, tumultuous assemblies, or local unorganized insurrections. However long may have been its previous conception, it nevertheless sprung forth suddenly from the parent brain, a Minerva in the full panoply of war. The President was bound to meet it in the shape it presents itself, without waiting for Congress to baptize it with a name; and no name given to it by him or them could change the fact.[57]

The court then went on to recognize that it was within the President's judgment to determine when the invasion or rebellion amounts to war and to decide on the defensive measures necessary to meet the challenge. In this respect the court stated:

Whether the President, in fulfilling his duties, as Commander-in-Chief, in suppressing an insurrection, has met with such armed hostile resistance, and a civil war of such alarming proportions, as will compel him to accord to them the character of belligerents, is a question to be decided *by him*, and this Court must be governed by the decision and acts of the political department of the government to which this power was entrusted. "He must determine what degree of force the crisis demands." The proclamation of blockade is itself official and conclusive evidence to the Court that a state of war existed which demanded and authorized a recourse to such a measure, under the circumstances peculiar to the case.[58]

It can readily be seen that the language of *The Prize Cases* in recognizing the power of the President to make defensive war and in placing that decision, as well as the determination as to the amount of force necessary, within his discretion in reality permits a presidential warmaking power with little or no restraint. It is true that he is confined to national self-defense and defensive measures only, but it would require little ingenuity to devise ways and means whereby an offensive or even an aggressive act is placed in the guise of defense.

A strong dissenting opinion written by Justice Nelson, noting the great changes that ensued in a nation's life in a shift from a state of peace to that of war, stressed the fact that the decision to make the change to a legal state of war should rest in the supreme or sovereign power, which in the United States would be the Congress. The dissenting opinion might well be more nearly in harmony with the intention of the framers of the Constitution, for it would nevertheless recognize that effective and speedy forceful action could be taken by the President in the face of a direct attack upon the nation. At this point there might be no time to resort to the Congress, and the President could act.

Nevertheless, he would be required to place the matter before the Congress as soon as possible, in order that his action could be ratified by a congressional declaration of war or by congressional authorization in some form. Congress, of course, under this viewpoint, could also refuse to ratify the presidential action; indeed, Congress could repudiate the action, although the point is quickly made that repudiation would be almost unthinkable in the face of a presidential action to meet an actual direct attack.[59] Consideration might also be given to the fact that re-

pudiation might well be dangerous to the nation and its safety. Repudi-
ating the President's action is not necessarily going to stop the attack,
and such repudiation might well weaken the President's ability to continue the defense.

The conclusion that the comprehensive opinion of *The Prize Cases*
amounts to a rejection of constitutional restrictions upon presidential
war-making would itself appear to be too all-encompassing. It is true
that the court places discretion with the President as to the hostile acts
which would compel him to act in defense and also as to the means
used to crush the attack, and concludes that such discretion is a power
entrusted to political departments of government and not to the judiciary. In stating that the question is political and not subject to judicial
check, the court is not stating that the president is not subject to constitutional limitation. It is simply stating that the matter is not a proper
subject of judicial restraint. It may well be that the President would be
subject to other restraint, for example a self-imposed restraint arising
from his oath to uphold the Constitution, or possibly impeachment and
conviction if he fails to uphold the Constitution. Thus, it behooves us
to inquire into legal doctrine in order to determine the extent of the
presidential power in an exercise of the inherent right of national self-
defense.

The framers spoke of a power to repel sudden attack, and the court
in *The Prize Cases* said that in case of rebellion or invasion of a foreign
nation the President can recognize that a state of war has been imposed
upon the United States and can wage it. Thus, in an exercise of the right
of national self-defense the President is constitutionally empowered to
defend the nation against an actual, direct, physical assault against the
territory of the United States. It is also assumed that the President would
not be forced to wait until the blow fell, but would be constitutionally
empowered to defend against an imminent attack by a preemptive
strike.[60]

The elements of legal self-defense in the concept of international
law were set out by Daniel Webster as secretary of state of the United
States, in the case of the *Steamer Caroline*.[61] In that case the *Caroline*,
located in United States waters while in the service of insurgents pre-
paring to attack Canada, was destroyed by a British force which made
a sudden incursion across the Niagara River. Webster, complaining of
the violation of the territory of the United States, declared in a note
to the British authorities that the inviolability of the territory of a state

may be held to yield to the right of self-defense in cases in which the necessity of self-defense was "instant, overwhelming, leaving no choice of means and no moment of deliberation."[62] In this view a state exercising the right of self-defense may do so in the face of an attack actual or impending and must show a danger direct and immediate. Following this definition of self-defense it can be implied that the President can act to repel an imminent impending attack.

Today, however, this viewpoint is subject to some doubt and controversy. The United Nations Charter, to which the United States, as a ratifying state, is legally bound, imposes the obligation on the members of the United Nations by the terms of Article 2(4) "to refrain in their international relations from the threat or use of force against the territorial integrity or political independence of any state or in any other manner inconsistent with the Purposes of the United Nations." This instrument does, however, permit the use of force in an exercise of the inherent right of individual and collective self-defense, at least until the Security Council takes the necessary measures to reestablish peace; but in speaking in terms of "inherent" right of self-defense, the Charter refers to it only in terms of action against armed attack. This gives rise to the question of whether the Charter seeks to define the inherent right of self-defense narrowly by limiting it to instances of armed attack. If this be the true meaning, the President would be limited in his defense of the nation to an instance of an actual armed attack and would be precluded from repelling an immediate anticipated attack.

It can be maintained that if self-defense is inherent, as Article 51 of the United Nations Charter says it is, it is inalienable, incapable of being surrendered—a natural right. If it is incapable of being surrendered in whole, it can be reasoned that it is incapable of being surrendered in part; therefore, in spite of the seeming limitation imposed, if it is truly inherent, the right of self-defense can still be resorted to wherever it is permitted under general international law, which would include action against an imminently threatened attack.[63]

Nevertheless, some jurists are of the opinion that the right of self-defense under the United Nations Charter is limited to action after an armed attack has occurred.[64] It is said that the use of the word "inherent" is of little significance legally speaking, for after using the word the Charter is not reverent of its legal meaning but apparently seeks to alter and change the general international law significance of self-defense. Moreover, it can be contended that positive law does not alter and change meanings even of so-called natural and unalterable rights. Thus it is concluded that the United Nations Charter does alter the right of self-defense as it existed at general international law, restricting it to instances where there has actually been an armed attack by an aggressor, and an imminent armed attack is not thought sufficient to invoke the right of self-defense under Article 51.

Issue has been taken with this severely limited view of the right of self-defense on the grounds that Charter interpretation does not necessarily warrant such a circumscribed conclusion. To the contrary, it is contended that the United Nations Charter does not change the right of self-defense as it existed at international law.[65] It is reasoned that Article 51 is only a declaratory article designed to preserve the right of self-defense, not to limit it, and containing no additional obligations.[66] It is then maintained that Article 2(4) is not inconsistent with the traditional right of self-defense, for interim measures taken by a state to protect and defend itself against an imminent threat of a use of force do not constitute a use of force against the territorial integrity or political independence of the state committing the delict and are not inconsistent with the purposes of the United Nations.[67]

From a more practical point of view, it is pointed out that the necessities of modern international life force a recognition by the international law of the United Nations Charter of a right of self-defense of broader scope, for to limit that right to armed attack in the absence of a truly effective collective security system could well circumscribe the legal right of a state to protect itself against its own destruction. A state can hardly be expected to wait for the start of an actual attack in the face of imminent threat of that attack, for if it did so the state might be so paralyzed by the attack that it could no longer render resistance.[68]

Nor could a President of the United States be expected under the Constitution of the United States to wait for the actual attack when imminently threatened. If he did so, he would fail in his duty to protect and defend the United States. There is evidence that the action of President John F. Kennedy and the Organization of American States in the Cuban missile crisis was predicated upon a right of self-defense against the clear and present danger emanating from the placing of missiles with nuclear capability in Cuba. President Kennedy stated that the actions were taken in defense of United States security and that of the Western Hemisphere.[69] Secretary of State Rusk spoke of the offensive nature of the weapons and stated that no country of the hemisphere could "feel secure from direct attack."[70]

It is further claimed by some jurists that self-defense at international law not only may be used against an illegal use of force or imminent threat thereof, but may extend to other delinquencies where it is exercised in a preventive and nonretributive manner. It is claimed that a state may legitimately resort to the right of self-defense for its protection when its essential rights are endangered by delictual conduct of another state. The danger to these rights must be unlawful; it must be serious and actual or so imminent that the necessity to resort to self-defense is instant and overwhelming. In addition, the exercise of the right is conditioned upon the absence of other lawful means of protection.

It is also argued that Article 51 does not prevent the exercise of the right of self-defense against delictual nonforceful conduct which endangers the security of a state, for as noted above, Article 51 was not intended to limit the traditional right of self-defense, and from a practical point of view a state cannot be expected to sit idly by in the face of illegal acts which jeopardize its security with no legal right to resort to self-defense when it cannot otherwise safeguard its rights.[71] Thus action taken in defense against another nation's delictual conduct in the form of economic aggression would be permissible. Economic aggression has been defined as measures of economic pressure taken by one state against another so as to violate its sovereignty and economic independence and threatening the base of its economic life. The manipulation of tariffs by one state, the imposition of embargoes and boycotts, the freezing of funds, can all be employed in such a way as to constitute economic aggression. Such illegal economic coercion then could justify an exercise of self-defense at international law if it jeopardizes the essential rights of a state which are requisite to its security.[72] Such reasoning would sustain a use of force against the Arab states if they deliberately employ the oil weapon as an economic instrument of coercion against the United States. If the employment of that weapon amounts to an illegality and an economic aggression, and if the essential security of the nation is endangered thereby, then a use of force might be considered legitimate under the United Nations Charter and by principles of general international law. Perhaps Secretary of State Kissinger was thinking in those terms when he refused to rule out a use of force if the oil weapon is used to strangle the industrialized world.[73]

Although a use of force under such circumstances might possibly be permitted by international law and the Charter, it would be difficult to argue its legality under United States constitutional doctrine. To do so, the framers' "repelling of sudden attack" would have to be extended to attack other than through a use of armed force, a type of attack which could hardly have been contemplated by them. *The Prize Cases* spoke in terms of the President's recognition of a war which had been thrust upon the United States by another state and his acting in the defense of the country.[74] The use of an economic weapon to coerce the United States could hardly be considered in terms of a war or an invasion.

Another problem created by the rationale of the framers, *The Prize Cases*, and the right of self-defense is that a presidential defense against attack is all that would be permitted. Thus it would seem that the President in meeting the attack must limit himself to defensive measures only. Authorities, however, differ on this point. Hamilton's position, as declared in answer to what some have interpreted as Jefferson's overly cautious defense stance in the Tripoli situation, has been interpreted broadly to mean that once the country is made subject to an attack, the executive may respond with all the force he sees fit to make use of. And even though his measures become measures of offense, they in effect remain defensive, so no declaration of war by the Congress is required.[75] This position would regard the President as having power not merely to take measures to meet the invasion, but to wage in full the war imposed upon the United States.

The belief of those with the other disagreeing view would be that the President does not have offensive but only defensive powers.[76] They admit, however, that the line would be a difficult one to draw. Nevertheless, they would feel that the president's power extends only to the securing of the nation from the attack. He can meet it and avert it only:

The nature of the Executive's defensive measures will depend upon the nature of the thrust, but at no time should this response be disproportionate to the assault. Should he be responding to nuclear attack, presumably there would be little or no distinction between defensive and offensive action— the exchange would be terminal for both parties. But should enemy submarines shell coastal cities with conventional ordnance, the President need only clear the coasts of the enemy ships; the launching of SAC and invasion of the enemy homeland ought to await congressional authorization. In sum, the Executive does not receive full war time powers simply because another state has directly assaulted American territory.[77]

Perhaps constitutional doctrine does not give a clear-cut answer to this problem, but international law and the United Nations Charter, which bind the nation, or which should bind the nation's executive, shed light on the issue. International law requires that self-defense not go beyond the necessity of averting the danger or suppressing the attack, and that it must cease after the needs of defense have been met. It must not be excessive, going no farther than it must to avert or suppress the attack.[78] Or to state it another way, the measures used must be reasonable, limited to averting the illegal danger to the safety of the wronged state and proportionate to that danger. These requirements of proportionality to the restrictions against unreasonableness and excessiveness should also apply to an exercise of the right of self-defense under the United Nations Charter.

The intention of the framers of the Constitution as well as the attitude of the Supreme Court in *The Prize Cases* makes evident the fact that a direct attack against the territory of the United States and its territorial possessions would warrant a presidential response with armed force in the defense of the nation. Would an armed attack by a state on American citizens living or stationed abroad justify a resort to a use of armed force by the President in order to protect and defend those citizens? Would an attack on United States ships or air or space craft operating outside the country justify a presidential response by force against the attacker in their defense? Such a broad presidential power under the Constitution has been questioned, but a position opposing such powers would appear to be too restrictive.

International law would recognize a right of self-defense in instances of attack not only against the territory of the state, but also against its citizens, its land, its sea, or its air forces. Indeed, such armed attacks against such targets have been characterized as armed aggression.[80] Traditional international law would include within the right of self-defense of a state the defense by a state of its nationals where attack was made against them and where the foreign state was unable or unwilling to protect them. This right of self-defense was grounded upon the notion that nationals of a state are an extension of the state itself and represent a part of the state that is as important as its territory, that an injury to its citizens is an injury to the state, and finally that an essential function of the state, indeed a reason for its being, is the protection of nationals.[81] This same extension of the right of self-defense can be applied to a state's armed forces, naval vessels, and air or space craft, for in protecting them the state would be defending its nationals in its military forces on land, at sea, and in the air.

The President of the United States has often acted to defend American lives when they have been subject to attack by governments or citizens of foreign states.[82] One of the latest of such instances was that which occurred in 1965 when civil strife erupted in the Dominican Republic.[83] During the first days of civil strife in that country, the situation rapidly degenerated into a state of anarchy, and there appeared to be little question but that the lives and limbs of citizens of the United States were seriously endangered. In such a situation, the original limited armed intervention by the United States as a last resort to prevent imminent and irreparable injury to its nationals would be legitimate, falling within a right of self-defense at traditional international law. Justification could also be made under the particular international law of the United Nations Charter, for despite a general prohibition of the use of individual armed force under that document, such use is recognized when made in the inherent right of self-defense.[84]

A more recent event which can be placed under a category of defense of citizens was the armed protection offered to the American merchant ship, *Mayaguez*, captured by Cambodians in 1975. In that instance a limited use of armed force was ordered by President Ford to free the ship and its crew. In a letter to the United Nations Secretary General and to the Security Council, President Ford invoked Article 51 of the United Nations Charter, which, of course, recognizes the inherent right of self-defense and a right to use armed force in its exercise.[85]

The President has the right to protect not only the lives of American citizens but also their property.[86] A use of force by the President to defend American property abroad is more difficult to justify under the Constitution and constitutional theory. It could hardly be concluded that the founding fathers would intend or the Supreme Court of the United States would conclude that the Constitution precluded a limited and proportionate forceful action by the President to protect and defend American lives from foreign armed attack. The protection of a state's citizens is an essential function of the state and, as noted, such citizens are an extension of the state itself, as important as the territory of the state. Thus, acting upon their behalf would be considered as defense of the state just as, under the reasoning of *The Prize Cases*, a defense of territory would be defense of the state.

It might seem farfetched to consider that private property located outside the United States, even though it belongs to American citizens, is an extension or a part of the nation, and that one of the nation's essential functions is to defend such property against foreign attack. Nevertheless, certain jurists have concluded that the protection of the property of nationals can at international law be said to fall within a right of self-defense[87] and that such a right has on many occasions been invoked by the government of the United States to justify United States action protective of the property.[88] If one assumes that delictual acts of one state that injure or endanger the security of another state give rise to a right of self-defense at international law, then, of course, protection against illegal attacks upon property by foreign nations could fall within the meaning of self-defense.[89] Even so, the use of force to protect the property of citizens could seldom be resorted to, for an attack against property would seldom endanger the security of the state. But if such security were at stake, then an international law right would come into existence. Can such a right be carried over into constitutional law so as to permit the President to use armed force to protect such property under an extended analogy to *The Prize Cases?* The theme running through *The Prize Cases* is that the President can act to defend the country against sudden attack. Thus he acts where the security of the nation so demands. One can therefore argue that in the unusual case where the attack on the property would endanger the nation's security, then the President might be authorized to act in a reasonable manner, limited to averting the illegal attack and the danger to the nation's safety, and with the understanding that his actions must be proportionate to that danger.

THEORY OF COLLECTIVE SELF-DEFENSE

Up to this point discussion has centered upon the President's constitutional power to resort to a use of force against a foreign power which has committed an armed attack or is imminently threatening such attack against the territory of the United States, its citizens, or its property. In modern times an extension of the concept of self-defense has occurred, and at international law there has been recognized not only a right of individual self-defense, but also a right of collective self-defense, i.e., states may not only act in self-defense when they are attacked, but they may take collective action in certain cases when other states are attacked in order to assist in the defense of such attacked states. Article 51 of the United Nations Charter recognizes a right to use armed force in an exercise of ". . . the inherent right of individual or collective self-defense if an armed attack occurs against a member of the United Nations, until the Security Council has taken the measures to maintain international peace and security." Building upon this, regional collective security pacts have been entered into by the nations of the world (such as the Inter-American Treaty of Reciprocal Assistance), wherein it is declared that an armed attack by a state against any state in the region shall be considered as an attack against all, and each state is given the right, if indeed not the duty, to assist the victim with defensive measures in meeting the attack.[90] Moreover, the right of collective self-defense has been maintained even in the absence of any regional agreement with a victim state.[91]

Since Article 51 of the United Nations Charter sanctions both a right of individual and of collective self-defense, can it be assumed that the President under the Constitution may act to protect or defend a foreign nation against an attack just as he may act in the nation's self-defense to protect the United States against attack? Such an assumption does not necessarily follow, and to a degree his constitutional power might depend upon a viewpoint adopted in relation to the so-called right of collective self-defense.

Collective self-defense is a term which has caused considerable controversy. By some it is considered a new term of international law, thought to be not collective self-defense but collective defense—i.e., that the Charter recognizes that a state subjected to attack has a right of self-defense and that other states have a right to come to its assistance.[92]

But one can reason that collective self-defense means no more than it means at general international law, i.e., that two or more states can take collective action in the right of self-defense when each has an individual right of self-defense.[93] For example, if State A has illegally attacked States B and C, both B and C could react in self-defense and the reaction could be in concert—collective self-defense. This, of course, presumes that both states have been direct victims of the delictual conduct. If only State B has been directly subjected, can State C ever aid State B in a right of self-defense, or would this be merely collective defense? To act in accord with self-defense, State C would have to show some legal interest of its own invaded by the action of State A. Within the concept of self-defense at municipal law there is recognized a limited right and a duty to protect others where a close relationship or kinship exists between certain parties, between, for example, the members of one's household, or in a situation where there is some special family relationship with the person defended. Extending by analogy this concept into the field of international law, the conclusion can be drawn that a state would be acting in self-defense when it defended another state having a legal right of self-defense where there existed a close relationship based upon solidarity, for the legal interests of both would be violated.[94] If the security of a group of states is dependent in fact upon the security of each and every one of them, a violation of the rights of any one of the group would be a violation of the rights of all, permitting joint effort for protection. Thus, one can reason that the United Nations Charter takes notice of the close integration and solidarity between certain nations and incorporates into international law the concept that each state has a legal right in the security of the actual victim; therefore, an aggression against one is equivalent to an aggression against the other nations integrated with it.

The argument has been made that *The Prize Cases* and the theory of self-defense considered therein could not be stretched to cover the repelling of an attack against the territory of another state.[95] This conclusion would appear to follow if collective self-defense is in reality collective defense. From a purely theoretical point of view, if this is the true meaning of collective self-defense one could hardly contend that a defense of another country is an action in self-defense of the defender. Practical difficulties also intrude. Should the President be considered as constitutionally authorized to repel an attack against any state of the world simply because such right of self-defense or defense might be recognized under the United Nations Charter? It is doubtful. The intent of the framers and the reasoning of the judges in *The Prize Cases* would recognize his right to repel sudden attack directly against the United States because the emergency situation would demand immediate response to protect the nation's security. To this all would agree, particularly when recognition is further given to the fact that the Congress could seldom act with sufficient speed to authorize the defense action in the form of a declaration of war or otherwise.

One would be hard put to say that an attack on any state of the world would so endanger the security of the United States as to permit the presidential action unless one accepts the broad amorphous idea, which is perhaps a cornerstone of universal collective security through international organization, that any aggression anywhere affects the security of all states and should be stopped—a sort of one-world type of thinking. This may be a basic notion of international peace and security organization, but United States constitutional theory can hardly be extended that far. In most situations of armed attack on another state, a decision would have to be made as to whether the security interests of the United States are so vitally at stake that such an attack demands and warrants immediate action to repel the attack for the defensive needs of the United States as well. Since the minds of men can reasonably differ as to the facts of the danger to United States security and, further, as to whether or not an immediate response is necessary to meet the danger, it would seem that the decision to initiate the war through a use of force should be with the Congress. To give the President carte blanche authority would come too close to giving him permission to initiate war. On the other hand, as has been noted, reasonable men would all agree that the security of the United States is affected when it is attacked and that an immediate response is needed to repel the attack to protect that security. In such an instance a congressional declaration of war would be pointless and the delay which such declaration might entail would be dangerous.[96]

If collective self-defense can in reality be viewed as collective self-defense, not collective defense, then it becomes more plausible to accept a view that presidential action on behalf of certain other countries could be regarded as constitutional and as an action in the nature of national self-defense. Certainly no problem would appear to arise if the United States is attacked and at the same time another state is attacked by the same attacker. The President could respond to repel the attack on the United States, and he could also act in concert with the other state to repel the attack. This could very well be accepted under the Hamiltonian position which permits the President to meet an attack against the United States and to take both defensive and offensive measures—in short, to wage in full the war which had been imposed upon the nation by the foreign attacker.[97]

But how about the second view of collective self-defense, i.e., that it refers to situations where there exists such a close relationship between the two states based on solidarity that right of collective self-defense is warranted? Here the legal interests of both states would be violated by an armed attack against either of them. If the security of a group of states (such as those bound together in the Organization of American States, the membership of which encompasses most of the states of the hemisphere, including the United States) is dependent in fact upon the security of each and every one of them, a violation of the rights of any member of the group would be a violation of the rights of all, permitting joint efforts of defense. The Charter of the Organization of American States[98] is based on the close integration and solidarity of the American Republics, and it and the Inter-American Treaty of Reciprocal Assistance[99] incorporate the concept that each state of the Americas has a legal right in the security of all other states of the Americas; an attack against one is said to be an attack against all. If an attack against any of the American states is an attack against all, then one can reason that the President would be justified in acting to repel, for example, a sudden attack against Mexico, for such would also be an attack against the United States. The very security of the United States has by the Inter-American Treaty been declared to be dependent upon the security of Mexico because of the two nations' close integration and solidarity. Their special relationship is set out in the Charter. This international legal integration has been accepted by all the nations involved. Thus it behooves the President to protect the security of the United States by aiding Mexico.

Although the expressions of solidarity, special relationship, and integration between and among the American countries are set forth in inter-American treaties, this is not meant to imply that a formal pact is necessary to create such a relationship. The special relationship in fact is that which is requisite, whether or not such a relationship is evidenced by an actual agreement. For example, even if no treaties existed between close friendly nations, such as the United States and Canada, it would be rather clearly obvious to legal commentators that a special relationship did exist between the two countries and that the security of each was dependent upon the security of the other. Thus a presidential action to defend Canada, if that nation were subject to sudden attack, could be justified in the same manner as a presidential action in defense of an attack on the United States would be justified. The security of the United States is in fact so bound up with that of Canada that its security would be vitally affected were Canada attacked.

Some issue has been taken, however, with this point of view. Although the fact of threat to the United States security is not questioned, still a difference has been noted. It has been pointed out that a communist invasion of Alaska would constitute the same threat to the security of the United States and its survival as would such an invasion of Canada.[100] It has been claimed, nevertheless, that the founding fathers would have sanctioned presidential action without congressional authorization in order to repel an attack against Alaska but not against Canada.

The reasoning in the case of Alaska is that presidential response is only to be permitted where there is a sudden attack, which because of military considerations would preclude congressional action, given the shortage of time. Moreover, congressional declaration of war would become of no importance, for war would have been foisted upon the United States by the direct attack against Alaska and the President would meet such a war by assuming the constitutional role of Commander-in-Chief.[101]

In an instance of attack on Canada, however, similar reasoning does not prevail. If a foreign nation, such as Canada, is attacked, war is not thrust upon the United States and the decision of United States involvement is said to be still open. Any decision to enter that war by the United States would be an initiation of war by the United States against the attacker. Since the decision for the initiation of war was intended to rest with the Congress, congressional declaration of war becomes requisite.[102]

This theory may be too technical for maintenance of the security of the United States. If the United States were closely bound up with Canada to the extent that an attack against Canada could in fact be considered an attack upon the United States, and if one could assume, as well might be the case, that in an instance of a direct attack against the United States there could be no question but that the security interests of the United States also demanded defense of Canada, then it would seem quite logical and permissible to assume that the President should be permitted to respond to a sudden attack against Canada, and indeed congressional action would become superfluous and militarily precluded in view of the need of immediate defense action.

The sustaining of this thesis which would uphold the presidential use of force upon an attack against another state in the absence of congressional authorization would appear to be dependent upon the presence of a proximate or special relationship in fact between the victim state and the defender. There would have been a violation not only of the victim's legal rights, but also of the defending state's rights which had been violated at the same time. Thus the protector is protecting its own legally recognized security interests, jeopardized by the attack on the victim, when it comes to the aid of the victim in an exercise of the right of collective self-defense. If such relationship between the two states is not present in fact, then in truth our collective self-defense becomes collective defense. If the President is acting in collective defense only, then his response, as seen above, is difficult to justify.

But even proceeding under what may be called true collective self-defense when the special relationship is requisite, the fact of the existence of the relationship is difficult to determine. For years a credo of faith has been that a proximate relationship based on solidarity between and among the American republics has existed, so that the security of all is dependent in fact upon the security of each. Thus if one is attacked, the legal rights of the others are also violated, giving rise to the right of self-defense. But is this dogma immutable? Speculations can be made as to whether the solidarity which would appear to sanction the relationship may today be shaky or completely absent. There has been a questioning as to whether there was in fact a proximate relationship between the United States and Vietnam, or indeed between the United States and Southeast Asia. It has been contended that the United States was not in reality a valid member of SEATO, that in effect it had no special solidarity with the peoples of the states of Southeast Asia, divided as they were from the United States by an ocean and not possessing historical or ethnic connections with the United States.[103] The United States government rejected the notion that such regional ties were needed, basing its ideas of collective self-defense on collective defense.[104] However, the critical feature which constitutes the relationship between states for purposes of collective self-defense is a common interest among the states, to the extent that they possess common security interests which lead them into a position whereby the maintenance of international peace and security in an area is essential for the security of all. Such common security interest in fact must be present; if it is, then it would seem that the President in the face of an attack upon a state must act to meet the attack in order to preserve the state's security and also that of the United States. The problem here arises as to whether United States security interests are in fact bound up with such states as Korea, Lebanon, or Vietnam. Perhaps United States security interests had already disappeared at the time of the Dominican Republic case. The solidarity of the Americas at the time of the use of force in that nation in an exercise of collective self-defense may no longer have existed. One can argue that the special relationship between the Dominican Republic and the United States was based on treaty, but a treaty cannot create a special relationship if in fact such a relationship does not exist.

THE COMMANDER-IN-CHIEF

In making the President the Commander-in-Chief of the armed

forces, the Constitution clothes him with a military function of great importance. It is he who commands the armed forces. As such a commander he, in time of war, whether that war be declared by the Congress or foisted upon the nation by the enemy, wages war. Congress declares but does not wage war. There is then no doubt as to his power to command the armed forces against the enemy in wartime.[105] Controversy does exist, however, as to his constitutional power to make use of the armed forces in time of peace when they are used in situations short of war. Can the Commander-in-Chief's power be interpreted as a fountain of power broad enough to permit a presidential use of force outside the United States for purposes short of war? As stated earlier, some authorities would view the Commander-in-Chief provision as one empowering the President to order the armed forces to go anywhere he wished and to do anything that could be done by such forces; there is really no practical restriction upon the power of the President to employ the armed forces as he sees fit.

Such an understanding of the Commander-in-Chief clause may well be too broad, and such a viewpoint is not in reality persuasive. Alexander Hamilton, writing in the *Federalist Papers*, saw only a limited amount of power delegated by the clause. He said that the President's power thereunder would ". . . amount to nothing more than the Supreme Command and direction of the military and naval forces . . ."[106] In directing those forces under him, a commander of military forces does not make the decision as to the political objectives or purposes which call for the employment of the forces. And, since the clause is silent regarding the purposes for which the President may act as Commander-in-Chief, then one must turn to other constitutional powers of the President to determine those purposes which may necessitate the employment of armed forces. Thus he must use his authority as Commander-in-Chief with the other buttressing constitutional powers.[107]

Constitutional theory and constitutional rationalizations which have been given for the military actions that have transpired in the past do not indicate that the clause in and of itself authorizes any military endeavor outside the shores of the United States.[108]

As we have seen, the President is plainly authorized to employ the military in times of war declared by Congress, or in the defense of the nation against invasion, or in order to suppress insurrection. Other executive powers have been cited, such as the foreign relations power of the President as well as his power faithfully to execute the laws.

As Commander-in-Chief the president may possibly also resort to these powers to support constitutionally a use of force externally against a foreign power.

FOREIGN RELATIONS POWER

Jurists have taken the position that the President's broad constitutional responsibilities over foreign affairs provide ample authority to sanction a presidential use of force, particularly when that authority is supplemented by his power as Commander-in-Chief.[109] Accordingly, when in his judgment the successful execution of the foreign policy of the United States demands the employment of armed force against a foreign state, then he is authorized to commit the armed forces to military operations. Such operations can range from military displays seeking to coerce the foreign state, to armed invasions and occupations as a means of preserving or advancing the foreign interests or relations of the nation.

It has been contended that the President's constitutional law right is subject to limitation by the Congress and that Congress is empowered to forbid the sending of troops outside the United States in pursuance of foreign policy goals, at least in time of peace. The late Professor Quincy Wright tells us quite clearly that

for the purpose of bringing pressure upon foreign governments for political objects, it is doubtful whether the President has constitutional power to use force although he may bring diplomatic pressure. For political intervention, authorization by special resolution of Congress seems proper and has been the usual practice.[110]

Others, however, view the right as a discretionary one vested in the President alone and thus not subject to the control of Congress, even though the exercise of the discretion and the presidential use of force might well result in war.[111]

American Presidents have clearly proceeded upon a belief that the chief executive possesses power to commit troops abroad to protect American foreign policy interests. Armed interventions have been directed against the political life of other countries to support one revolutionary faction over another. Intervention has been carried out in Latin America to prevent European intervention and occupation of those countries in the belief that such would be detrimental to United States interests. In a crusading spirit the United States has intervened on occasion to impose a democratic republican form of government in foreign states.[112]

It has been said that the consent of Congress should be obtained by the President if the purpose behind the use of force is political; that is, if it is used to support diplomatic moves against a foreign state, to acquire territory from a foreign state or to occupy or invade that territory, or to influence the political life or ideology of a foreign nation.[113] Such a use of force against another sovereign state, it is contended, is an intervention to change the condition of things therein and is pregnant with legal and moral effects and outcomes. Actually, such use of force should not be resorted to at all under international law, for that body of law makes intervention for such purposes illegal. At general international law, armed intervention is considered legitimate only when taken in an exercise of the right of self-defense, as discussed above, when exercised as a sanction against a state violator of international law by the state which has been injured by the delict, or when the intervention is taken with the consent of a state.[114] The latter should not be called intervention, for intervention is defined as actions taken against the will of the intervened state.[115] An action taken purely to advance the foreign relations policies of the United States could hardly be considered legitimate.

The particular law of the United Nations Charter proscribes the use of armed force even more drastically. That Charter's main purpose is to eliminate the threat or use of force, whether it be a lawful or unlawful use of force under general international law by individual members, except in self-defense or as a step in the participation of collective sanctions laid down by the Security Council. It commands members to ". . . refrain in their international relations from the threat or use of force against the territorial integrity or political independence of any state, or in any other manner inconsistent with the purposes of the United Nations." Therefore, if the United States is to engage in an armed intervention in a foreign nation to protect only its political interests, and by so doing will commit a breach of international law, it is thought that such derogation from law with its serious consequences should have the support of Congress. The peoples' will as expressed through their representatives in the legislative branch should prevail.[116]

THE DUTY FAITHFULLY TO EXECUTE THE LAWS

The Constitution of the United States places upon the President the obligation faithfully to execute the laws,[117] and the laws which he is called upon to execute are not confined to statutes enacted by the Congress. The Constitution is itself law.[118] In *The Slaughter House Cases*[119] the court held that the privileges and immunities of national citizenship comprised among other things a right of citizens to protection abroad. Consequently, in order to effectuate national privileges and immunities the President would be authorized to use armed force if necessary as Commander-in-Chief for the purpose of protecting endangered citizens abroad. It is true that the privileges and immunities clause of the fourteenth amendment is addressed to the states of the union and restricts their violations of national privileges and immunities only. Nevertheless, the case of *Crandall v. Nevada*[120] tells us that those privileges and immunities exist even in the absence of the express wording of the fourteenth amendment, and as these rights are existent they are subject to protection. It is also true that the fourteenth amendment's fifth section speaks of enforcement of its provisions by the Congress through appropriate legislation, but as pointed out in *Crandall*, privileges and immunities of national citizenship emanate from the contours of the Constitution and the necessities of the nation. No language exists in the case one way or another that concerns the enforcement of such privileges and immunities or that speaks of Congress as the enforcing agency. It would therefore stand to reason that the President would by inference be empowered to enforce such privileges; and since the President is not limited to the enforcement of statutes only, but may also enforce rights and obligations arising out of the Constitution itself, he would be constitutionally authorized to use force to safeguard a privilege and immunity of national citizenship, i.e., the protection of endangered citizens abroad.[121] Moreover, the constitutionality of presidential action to defend the lives of American citizens abroad can also be, as seen earlier, based on self-defense.[122] Such action can also be grounded upon the enforcement of international law, for at general international law a denial of justice by a state in its treatment of citizens of other states has been considered a delict violative of international law.[123]

Presidential power to execute the law has been extended to the faithful execution of customary international law. Since the early days of the nation, federal and state courts have declared that international law is a part of the law of the land. As early as 1784, the chief justice of the Supreme Court of Pennsylvania declared that a case before the court was to be decided according to "principles of the law of nations which form a part of the municipal law of Pennsylvania."[124] Later in *The Paquete Habana* the Supreme Court of the United States assured:[125] "International law is part of our law and must be ascertained and administered by the courts of justice of appropriate jurisdiction as often as questions of right depending upon it are duly presented for their determination."[126]

Alexander Hamilton, writing as Pacificus, reaffirmed such a thesis when speaking of the President as "the constitutional *EXECUTOR* of the laws." He went on to say: "Our treaties and the law of nations form a part of the law of the land."[127]

The Supreme Court of the United States in an indirect manner and by way of dictum has recognized that the President's duty faithfully to execute the laws would also include a duty to enforce international law and treaties. In the 1890 case of *In re Neagle*[128] the court queried:

Is this duty limited to the enforcement of Acts of Congress or of treaties of the United States according to their express terms, or does it include the rights, duties and obligations growing out of the Constitution itself, our international relations and the protection implied by the nature of the government under the Constitution?[129]

It becomes clear from reading the case that the duty includes the obligations growing out of the Constitution as well as out of international relations.

Earlier in 1860 an opinion by Supreme Court Justice Nelson, sitting on circuit in a lower federal court, confirmed the right of the executive to use force abroad for the protection of the rights of life, liberty, and property of Americans abroad. It was said that the decision to engage in such forceful interposition for the purpose indicated was within the discretion of the President:

Acts of lawless violence, or of threatened violence to the citizen or his property, cannot be anticipated and provided for; and the protection to be effectual or of any avail, may, not unfrequently, require the most prompt and decided action.[130]

The circumstances which prompted this case and its decision had to do with an American bombardment of Greytown, Nicaragua. The authorities there had failed to comply with an ultimatum issued by a naval captain which required that an apology be extended to an American consul who had suffered indignities, and that reparation be made to an American company whose property had been destroyed. The captain was acting under orders of the President and the secretary of the navy.[131]

As we have noted previously, the protection of citizens abroad may in certain instances be justified under the Constitution in terms of national privilege or immunity, or as a right of national self-defense recognized by the Constitution and by international law. Self-defense, however, is not designed to enforce or vindicate the law. It seeks to avert an unlawful danger to the rights of citizens abroad, and action for protection must cease after the needs of defense have been met.[132] Protection of the rights of citizens abroad may be of broader extent, and the action might be taken as a sanction or reprisal. Reprisals or sanctions may be general retaliatory measures of a coercive nature, even involving the use of armed force, taken for a violation of international law by the state injured in order to secure reparation or to prevent a recurrence of unlawful acts or omissions of the delinquent state.[133] Such action is a form of self-help to enforce or vindicate the law, to punish the delinquent, and to secure redress. Thus international law has recognized that a state is called upon to treat an alien in such a way as to accord with civilized standards of justice. If its treatment falls below this standard respecting the alien's life, liberty, or property, then a right of intervention against the delinquent state has been recognized as legally justifiable by the state of citizenship of the alien in order to protect the citizen abroad. Such action then could be taken to secure reparation for the illegal offense, to force a return to legality, and to avoid new offenses.[134]

Following the language of the *Neagle* case, therefore, the President would simply be enforcing international law when he ordered a use of force short of war for the protection of United States citizens in a state where their rights were violated to an extent also violative of international law. This would then be a constitutional responsibility of the President. He would simply be faithfully executing the law of the United States, which is inclusive of international law.[135] Quincy Wright states it well: "For the meeting of responsibilities under international law and treaty the President likewise has authority to use the army and navy on the high seas and in foreign territory."[136]

It has been contended that it would be permissible for the President to authorize a neutral use of force simply to protect citizens in a foreign state which did not interfere with the political life of the intervened state. Quantitatively this would involve only a minor use of force, and since the sole purpose of the use of force would be to protect the rights of citizens in accordance with international law, moral or legal consequences would not be involved, as would be the case if the force were used to interfere with the political life of the nation. The President could order the use of force in this instance, for the congressional war-declaring power is based on other criteria, namely, to assure that the will of the people be represented when physical and economic sacrifice of large magnitude ensued and where vast legal and vital, moral, foreign-relations resultants were involved.[137] The State Department's solicitor apparently took this position in 1912. After discussing political interventions such as those taken in local political affairs of another country to support or change its government, the author stated that intervention for the protection of citizens was nonpolitical, its sole motive being to protect said citizens

either from the acts of the government itself or from the acts of persons or bodies of persons resident within the jurisdiction of a government which finds itself unable to afford the requisite protection until the government concerned is willing or able to afford the protection. When this is accomplished the interposing state withdraws, leaving the government either as it found it or as it may have been altered by purely internal and local means, with which matters the interposing government has had no interest, concern, or connection.[138]

These words sound more like the protection of the citizens as an exercise of a right of self-defense, as would be exemplified by the United States–Belgian action in the Congo when the armed forces were used to rescue citizens. The military planes flew in, landed, and rescued the citizens. They then flew out, leaving no imprint upon the political life of the country.[139]

When armed forces remain to obtain reparation or to force a return to legality, the neutrality would go out the window, for almost of necessity interference in the political life of the country would come about.

Armed force has also been directed by the President against nations which have breached other rules of international law so as to injure the United States. Force was used at various times to suppress piracy and the slave trade, both recognized as illegal by international law. Marines were sent into nations not only to protect American lives but also to enforce the right of legation when attacks had been made on those legations.[140] These enforcements of international law might be characterized as a neutral use of force, although in the case where the United States sent forces into China in 1900 to protect the right of legation endangered by the Boxer rebellion, the foreign forces bolstered the corrupt Manchu regime, thus preserving it against its political enemies in China.[141] This would be something more than nonpolitical.

In any event, it would appear that sanctions taken by individual states are now outlawed by the United Nations Charter, the main purpose of which is to eliminate the use or threat of force, whether it be lawful or unlawful use of force under general international law, by individual members[142] except in self-defense[143] or as a step in the participation in collective measures laid down by the Security Council.[144] Thus the right of self-help in the form of forceful sanctions or reprisals has been restricted by the particular international law of the Charter.[145] The President then can hardly say that he is faithfully executing international law by an action which customary or particular international law declares to be illegal.

This latter statement would indicate that the President acts unconstitutionally when he breaches the law of nations. Such a thesis is a highly controversial one and subject to disagreement among jurists. There is no clear-cut United States Supreme Court authority, expressed or by way of dicta, supporting a view that the President is constitutionally obligated to follow and obey international law even when executing the principles and rules of that law. Professor Henkin, after telling us that international law has been incorporated into the law of the United States and that it is law which is to be applied by both the courts and the executive, still declares bluntly that violation of such law or of an international treaty by the President or by the Congress in the carrying out of their constitutional powers is not forbidden by the Constitution.[146]

He cites certain Supreme Court cases in which it has been concluded that international law would be applied, but only if the matter at hand was not controlled by an act of Congress.[147] In *The Paquete Habana*, where it was stated that international law was incorporated into the law of the nation, it was made most clear that the courts would give effect to the law of nations but only "in the absence of any treaty or other public act of their own government in relation to the matter."[148] Even more clearly it was added that the Supreme Court would follow customary international Law "where there is no treaty, and no controlling executive or legislative act or judicial decision."[149] Chief Justice Marshall reasoned in a similar fashion,[150] but he did say that "an act of Congress ought never to be construed to violate the law of nations, if any other possible construction remains."[151]

Justice Story reached a differing conclusion. He recognized that a certain discretion rested in the President as to the manner and extent of his actions in time of war; still he could not "lawfully transcend the rules of warfare established among civilized nations."[152] Here illegality would be presented through a violation of the law of nations. Professor Henkin suggests that the illegality would exist only under international law, and that Justice Story possibly did not mean to infer a constitutional infraction but an international infraction through the failure to follow international law.[153]

During the Vietnam conflict a polemic occurred between two noted internationalists on the matter of presidential war-making powers. Professor Richard Falk was of the opinion that the President was empowered by the Constitution to use armed force in Vietnam without a congressional declaration of war, but only if the action taken accorded with international law. He also considered the issue of presidential violation of international law to be a constitutional one. In his words: "The President is bound to act in accord with governing law, including international law. The customary and treaty norms of international law enjoy the status of 'the law of the land' and the President has no discretion to violate these norms in the course of pursuing objectives of foreign policy."[154] This premise would correspond to Justice Story's position, if we can assume that he was speaking of constitutional law rather than international law as the law to which the President's commitments of armed force should correspond.

Professor John N. Moore took issue with this viewpoint, declaring strongly that it was erroneous. He pointed out that Falk had set forth no authority to support his view. Stating that Congress and the President both exercise foreign-relations power, Moore noted that nothing seems to indicate that they act unconstitutionally when they violate norms of international law. Indeed, he pointed to the fact that the Supreme Court has held that a congressional statute enacted later in time than a treaty which conflicts therewith overrides the treaty. Such an override would be constitutional even though the congressional action would violate international law. One should also note that repudiations of treaties by the President have occurred even though such repudiations can well be considered a violation of international law, unless permitted by the treaty or by some countervailing rule of international law itself.[155]

Professor Falk, in rejoinder to Professor Moore, admitted that there was no established legal doctrine obligating the President to obey international law. The question was said to be an open one. He went on to opine "that it seems reasonable to contend that this is the way the Constitution ought to be authoritatively construed."[156]

The thesis that the President is constitutionally obligated to obey the norms of international law is somewhat broader perhaps than the contention that is made here, i.e., that international law as part of the law of the land is to be faithfully executed, and by the use of force if necessary, so that a declaration of war or other congressional authorization would not be constitutionally necessary. Such a use of force for such a purpose is constitutionally authorized by the Constitution and by constitutional interpretation. Further, it is postulated that such use of force in violation of international law would amount to a violation of the Constitution, for in such an instance the President would no longer be acting within his constitutional power; he would not be faithfully executing the laws among which is international law.

The whole issue, however, is largely hypothetical and abstract, for the President would probably never admit that he was committing a violation of international law when he was enforcing it through a use of arms. Moreover, it is believed that the courts and the Supreme Court of the United States in the last analysis would refuse to hear a case or controversy if one ever arose again, for the political-question doctrine would prevent such a hearing.[157] This, however, in no wise reduces the President's constitutional responsibility faithfully to execute the laws, including international law, without violation thereof. For if he fails to execute the laws faithfully, he violates his oath to uphold the Constitution.

Treaties

Treaties of military alliance have long been a recognized feature of the international scene, that is, those treaties by which each signatory commits itself to come to the aid of other signatories in case any one of them is subjected to attack. Even before the entry into effect of the present Constitution, a treaty of alliance with France provided that if war occurred between Britain and France during the continuance of the revolutionary war, France and the United States would make common cause and would aid each other with mutual action, including the use of armed force.[158] Throughout the early history of the United States such bilateral treaties of alliance, or mutual defense treaties, were scarce, but in recent times they have multiplied. For example, the bilateral Mutual Defense Treaty between the United States and the Republic of China, which became effective in 1955, provides: "Each Party recognizes that an armed attack in the Western Pacific area directed against the territories of either of the Parties would be dangerous to its own peace and safety and declares that it would act to meet the common danger in accordance with its constitutional processes."[159]

Since World War II, the United States has entered into a number of multilateral collective security or defense treaties with various states of the world. The Inter-American Treaty of Reciprocal Assistance[160] binds each of the member American states to assist in meeting an attack against an American state in the exercise of the right of individual and collective self-defense, for such attack is considered an attack against all the American states. An organ of consultation is empowered to call upon each of the members to take certain collective measures necessary to meet the attack, as well as measures necessary for the peace and security of the continent in case of aggressions against an American state which are not armed attacks, and also in cases of other facts or situations endangering the peace of the Americas. Such measures can include the use of armed force, although no state can by order of the organ be forced to use armed force against its will.

The North Atlantic Treaty[161] contains similar provisions. It also declares that an armed attack against any of its members in Europe or in the North Atlantic area shall be considered an attack against all. It is further agreed that in case of such an armed attack, each member will aid the member attacked by taking ". . . such action as it deems necessary including the use of armed force."

The Southeast Asia Treaty Organization[162] (SEATO) and other collective defense agreements to which the United States is a party contain similar language. Indeed, the SEATO pact has been utilized as a partial basis for the United States intervention in Vietnam and for the legality of the intervention. The signatories of that treaty agreed that an armed attack against any of the parties within the Southeast Asia region or against any other state within it which the parties unanimously designate would, if attacked, endanger each party's peace and safety. Thus it was stated that each party would in the event of an armed aggressive attack ". . . meet the common danger in accord with constitutional processes."[163] An annex to the treaty stated that Cambodia, Laos, and the State of Vietnam were unanimously designated as states within the region, an attack upon which would obligate the parties to meet the common danger. The United States claimed that it was obligated by these provisions to meet an armed attack upon South Vietnam.[164]

Since the days of the ill-fated League of Nations, doubts have been prevalent and expressed as to the constitutionality of a treaty commitment which obligates the United States to wage and initiate war, such treaty authorization being viewed as in effect taking from the Congress its exclusive power to declare war, and in effect also authorizing the President to take such necessary forceful action as might be called for by the treaty. It has been argued that the power to initiate war is vested exclusively in the two houses of Congress and to permit the President to do so by treaty, which requires approval by only one house, the Senate, would do violence to the Constitution.[165] The appropriation power is also said to be vested exclusively in the Congress, and despite contentions that a treaty could by itself authorize appropriations, authority generally is in disagreement. An appropriation must be approved by both houses of Congress over and above the treaty authorization.[166] Nevertheless, it should be pointed out that the President and the Senate alone have acted by treaty in other areas of congressional power—for example, the control of foreign commerce—so that there has come to be a sharing by the President with the Senate.[167]

The consensus seems to be that the treaty-making power is broad enough to permit a treaty to be entered into with a foreign nation or nations committing the United States to the use of force and the declaration and waging of war, under certain stated treaty circumstances.[168] But the initiation and declaration of war when those circumstances come into being would still be subject to the will of the Congress, for the agreement to declare war and its actual declaration and initiation are differing things. The latter are exclusively within the powers of the Congress. It will be remembered that the framers considered giving to the Senate alone the power to declare war, but this was rejected and the power was given to the whole legislative body. Therefore it can hardly be argued that the President and Senate through a treaty could initiate a war.[169]

Nevertheless, it will further be remembered that not every use of force brings about a state of war. Congressional action is necessary only to initiate a legal state of war. Armed force amounting to a material war can be carried on by the President if authorized by his constitutional powers. Too, the President may wage war by accepting the challenge of an act of war or use of force against the United States. Here he does not initiate the war. That is done by the other state. He merely acts in self-defense.[170]

Thus those treaties binding the United States to act in a right of individual and collective self-defense are not necessary to augment presidential power to meet the attack; and this is true, as we have seen,[171] when the attack is against a foreign nation if the attack is also considered against the security of the United States.

Under the Rio Treaty, however, the members, including the United States, may be called upon to act and use armed force if recommended by the Organ of Consultation in instances of aggression not an armed attack against an American state, or in other instances which endanger the peace of the Americas.

It would seem that the doctrine of *The Prize Cases* is confined to the meeting of an attack involving the use of force, or at least imminent threat thereof. This would be the extent of the President's power in an exercise of the right of self-defense, as envisaged by the opinion of the court in *The Prize Cases*. Nevertheless, he could act to implement a decision of the Organ of Consultation that collective armed force had become requisite to meet the aggression or other peace-endangering act not involving a use of armed force, on the constitutional ground of enforcing a treaty to which the United States is a part. Under the Constitution of the United States, a treaty is said to be, along with the Constitution and the federal laws, the supreme law of the land. In carrying out the treaty, the President is simply faithfully executing a part of the nation's law. It can also be reasoned that he is enforcing international law, for that demands *pacta sunt servanda* (treaties must be kept in good faith). By executing the terms of the treaty, the President is following the international law command and faithfully executing such law in accord with this basic principle. The use of force would perforce have to be short of a legal state of war, which can be initiated only by Congress.

Implementation by the United States of the obligations to provide and to use armed force under the United Nations Charter have been said to create something of a special problem. Article 42 of the Charter provides that certain enforcement measures, even involving the use of armed force, can be ordered by the Security Council in instances when aggression, threats to the peace, or breaches of the peace have occurred. The armed forces to be used as contemplated by Article 43 of the Charter were forces made available to the Security Council in accordance with special agreements. As to United States troops which were to be placed at the disposal of the Council, an act of Congress, called the United Nations Participating Act, provided that any special agreement negotiated by the President respecting the number and type of armed forces to be made available to the United Nations had to be submitted to Congress for its approval.[172] It may be that this restricts the constitutional power of the President to make executive agreements, and thus treads unconstitutionally upon executive power. On the other hand, there would be no question but that the act of Congress also bolsters the presidential power, so that when he acts with Congress all doubt as to the constitutional commitment of troops by the Security Council would be resolved.

In any event, this restriction is not of great import, for the act does not require the authorization of the Congress when the President makes available to the Security Council the armed forces, facilities, or assistance provided. The actual furnishing of the armed forces pursuant to the special agreement is left in presidential hands. The President orders the force to fulfill the obligation. The whole matter is moot at the present time, for no special agreements as contemplated by the United Nations Charter have ever been entered into between the Security Council and the members of the United Nations. When the invasion of South Korea occurred, the United Nations reacted by calling the attack a breach of the peace and by recommending that members furnish assistance to South Korea to repel the armed attack.[173] Later another resolution recommended that members make military force and other assistance available to a unified United Nations command.[174] In this manner, the Security Council was legally able to place armed forces in the fields, even though the military agreements contemplated under Article 43 were not in existence.

President Truman committed United States armed forces to assist Korea prior to the passage of the last-mentioned Security Council resolution. Although the action could probably have been legally based on the right of collective self-defense, that right under Article 51 of the Charter was not invoked. Instead the President stated that he acted to support the first Security Council Resolution, which requested that each state give assistance to South Korea. Moreover, the principles and purposes of the Charter were cited.[175] The President's commitment of United States troops was then based on the implementation of these resolutions of the Security Council, which were authorized by the United Nations Charter. The United Nations Participation Act was not relevant here. No military agreements which it contemplated had been negotiated or concluded. The President was acting to carry out a recommendation of the Security Council which had nothing to do with military agreements necessary to implement Article 43. He was acting to fulfill the obligation of an international treaty, the United Nations Charter.

It has been contended, however, that since the President acted under a mere recommendation of the Security Council, as distinguished from a binding decision of that body, he should have obtained congressional authorization. Moreover, the very magnitude of the Korean venture and the fact that it was not a neutral intervention would indicate that this was the type of armed situation that the founding fathers would have held to be committed to congressional war-declaring power.[176] Nevertheless, authority both in practice and in law indicate the contrary, so that the President is empowered to use force short of legal war to implement and execute a treaty to which the United States is a party.[177]

The same can be said to be true of recommendations of the General Assembly under the Uniting for Peace Resolution.[178] The President would be legally empowered to implement such recommendations. It has been stated that military measures which the General Assembly could authorize by recommendation would be measures that members could take on their own under the Charter in the exercise of the right of collective self-defense under Article 51.[179] Here, of course, the President would be acting under his legal authority to defend the security of the nation.

It would then seem that treaties can commit the nation to a future use of armed force and that the enforcement or execution of the treaty, being part of the President's power faithfully to execute the laws, can be carried out by him through a use of armed force short of war. Can the same thing be said of an executive agreement which the President enters into with a foreign state, but which he does not submit to the Senate for approval as a treaty? Treaties and executive agreements have been employed interchangeably in our foreign affairs, and the constitutional power of the President to make them on his sole authority has been upheld by the Supreme Court of the United States.[180] On the international scene and at international law, executive agreements are as binding as treaties. Nevertheless, a mutual security or defense arrangement with a foreign state or states which would call for a use of armed force has been criticized when made by executive agreement.[181] It is contended that since its implementation may require a congressional declaration of war, the agreement should at least be presented in treaty form for Senate approval.[182] Such agreements have, however, been made by the President, and it can be concluded from legal analogy that they are valid and binding upon the President and that they authorize his use of armed force upon the arising of the conditions set forth in the agreement. As we have noted, they are considered binding at international law, and the Supreme Court has stated that international law is a part of the law of the United States to be faithfully executed by the President. If he uses force short of legal war according to the terms of the agreement, he is merely doing what the Constitution demands, for he is faithfully executing the law. Moreover, if the security of the United States was in reality involved by the attack on the other party, then the President could act even though there was no executive agreement. He would be acting to protect and defend the United States.[183]

Finally, there are other types of international agreements, which may be in the form either of a treaty or of an executive agreement, by the terms of which a state has been given the right to intervene in another state with armed force when certain circumstances exist in that state. The United States has on many occasions entered into agreements with other states which permit United States armed forces to be stationed within that state's territory. Clearly this would appear to be constitutional, particularly when supplemented with the Commander-in-Chief power and the power over foreign relations. If the consent of the host state is freely given, there is no problem of war or of fighting with the host country, and thus it can hardly be argued that the consent of the Congress is needed.

However, other agreements have been made in the past with Caribbean and Central American countries which provided for United States armed intervention in order to maintain a government in those countries adequate for the protection of life, property, and individual liberty.

Usually the United States interventions which took place in pursuance of these agreements were undertaken in time of rebellion and disorder for the purpose of maintaining internal peace and stable government.[184] Such an intervention could also be required by a government of a state beset by civil strife, in the absence of any prior formal agreement. In either event the armed intervention would be said to be based on the consent of the state. The legality of consent to armed intervention by another state given by a government of a state in time of civil strife is subject to some doubt. Some would say that if in fact serious civil strife exists in a state, consent by the government could hardly be called the consent of the state, for the very fact of the civil strife would show that the identity of the legal representative of the state was in doubt. An agreement for intervention in such a situation would not be lawful at international law, for it would be made without the acquiescence of a large number of the state's citizens. And the President could not claim constitutional power to execute an agreement invalid at international law.[185]

Others, however, would disagree, holding that the duties of foreign governments are owed to the legitimate government, and until a state of actual civil war comes into being neutrality as between the contending factions, government and rebels, is not required. Aid to the government in a state of civil strife which has not ripened into all-out civil war is permitted, but aid to the rebels is not. If this be the correct interpretation of international law, the President could act constitutionally, for he would be enforcing a valid international agreement.

But what if the prior consent to the armed intervention was given in accord with the free will of the state when no civil strife existed? So long as that consent continues, of course, there is no unlawful intervention. But what if civil strife breaks out and the President intervenes to aid the legitimate government, and that government freely consents to the intervention to maintain itself in power? This presents a quandary. The President is acting in accordance with a valid treaty, carrying out its terms in accord with principles of *pacta sunt servada*, and thus he is enforcing a United States treaty and international law. Only if in some way the state withdrew its consent could it be argued that the intervention would be illegal at international law. Even if by refusing the consent the states breached the treaty, still a landing of forces within the state would amount to illegal intervention without consent, illegal under the non-intervention principle. Under that principle a state no longer has a legal right to take reprisals to enforce an international treaty or international law.[186] Thus the President could not be acting constitutionally to execute the law. Query: does the fact of civil strife withdraw the state's consent to intervene on the side of one faction or another?

CONGRESSIONAL AUTHORIZATION

Popular opinion usually concludes that where congressional authorization is requisite for a constitutional commitment of troops to combat, nothing less than a formal congressional declaration of war will do. Nevertheless, military history[187] and what little judicial precedent[188] exists point the other way, and it seems rather clear that a formal congressional declaration of war is not necessary to express the consent of Congress to military action of a warlike nature. In 1967 a Senate committee stated: "The Committee does not believe that formal declarations of war are the only available means by which Congress can authorize the President to initiate limited or general hostilities."[189] Following this line of thought, the District of Columbia Circuit Court said:

We are unanimously agreed that it is constitutionally permissible for Congress to use other means than a formal declaration of war to give its approval to a war such as is involved in the protracted and substantial hostilities in Indo-China. See Massachusetts v. Laird and Orlando v. Laird, both *supra*.[190]

The nation's history bears ample proof of the conduct of military activity without formal declaration. Resort has not been made to formal declaration since World War II. This has probably resulted from the fact that war, under the United Nations Charter, is now considered to be illegal. Further, a failure to declare war permits an avoidance of the full-scale consequences of war at international law on neutrals and belligerents alike.[191]

Even though formal declaration of war may not be constitutionally required, still lesser modes of congressional authorization have also been subjects of contention as to constitutionality. An express authorization or approval of presidential military action may take place through joint or concurrent resolution, and in recent years such resolutions have been a principal method of congressional approval of the use of military force abroad. Undersecretary Katzenbach has called this type of congressional resolution "a functional equivalent of the declaration of war."[192] This type of resolution does indicate congressional assent to the conduct of the war, and thus would seemingly meet the intention of the constitutional fathers in placing the power to approve the carrying on of war in the Congress.[193] Nevertheless, such resolutions have been considered unconstitutional by some as predeclarations of war; as blank checks made to the order of the President to engage in hostilities as he sees fit; as rubber stamps of warlike action already committed; or as unconstitutional declarations to the executive of the congressional power to declare war.[194]

Classical constitutional doctrine tells us that Congress cannot delegate its authority to others. Still, the courts have permitted grants to the executive and to administrative agencies of considerable discretionary authority to implement and execute broadly stated congressional policies and objectives. The Supreme Court has set forth the requirement that a congressionally fixed, intelligible standard should be delineated by the Congress to control the delegated party's discretion.[195]

The congressional resolution of 1955 regarding Formosa,[196] that of 1957 regarding the Middle East,[197] and that of the Tonkin Gulf[198] have all been criticized as unconstitutional delegations of the war-declaring power because sufficient criteria to govern the presidential discretion to go to war were said not to be present. The Formosa resolution authorizes the President

to employ the Armed Forces of the United States as he deems necessary for the specific purpose of securing and protecting Formosa and the Pescadores against armed attack; this authority to include the securing and protecting of such related positions and territories of that area now in friendly hands and the taking of such other measures as he judges to be required or appropriate in assuring the defense of Formosa and the Pescadores.

The Middle East Resolution was taken to preserve the independence and integrity of Middle Eastern states. It declares: "To this end, if the President determines the necessity thereof, the United States is prepared to use armed forces to assist any nation or group of nations requesting assistance against armed aggression from any country controlled by international communism. . . ." The Tonkin Gulf Resolution approves the determination of the President "to take all necessary measures to repel any armed attack against the forces of the United States and to prevent further aggression." It then goes on to say that in conformity with the Constitution of the United States, the United Nations Charter, and the Southeast Asia Treaty, "The United States is . . . prepared as the President determines to take all necessary steps, including the use of force to assist any member or protocol state of the Southeast Asia Collective Defense Treaty requesting assistance in defense of its freedom." It is claimed that in these three instruments the power to make the decision to use armed force is left in the discretion of the President, and therefore the lack of standard fixed by the Congress makes for an unconstitutional delegation of power.[199]

The Supreme Court of the United States has permitted the Congress to delegate broad discretionary authority to the executive, and for the most part the court has been little troubled by the delegation barrier, in cases of domestic economic regulation.[200] Furthermore, in the field of foreign affairs, broad grants of power to the President have been sustained. Justice Sutherland's opinion in *United States v. Curtiss-Wright Export Corporation*[201] would lead us to believe that the delegation of powers doctrine is inapplicable to congressional delegation in the field of external affairs, because of the federal government's inherent power in the area and the President's autonomous authority in dealing with such affairs.

It has been suggested that *Curtiss-Wright* paints too broadly.[202] But even if some congressional standard should be required in external affairs, the President can still act without congressional delegation wherever he has an autonomous constitutional authority.[203] Where he does have such autonomous power, for example in an exercise of the right of self-defense or in carrying out a proper directive of the United Nations, a broad delegation or even no delegation of authority so to act would appear to be sufficient.

In any event, circuit courts have concluded that congressional authorization and support of the Vietnam conflict can be gathered from the Gulf of Tonkin Resolution. In *Orlando v. Laird* the court said that

the resolution was expressed in broad language which clearly showed the state of mind of the Congress and its intention fully to implement and support the military and naval actions taken by and planned to be taken by the President at that time in Southeast Asia, and as might be required in the future "to prevent further aggression."[204]

The question of congressional acquiescence in presidential commitments of armed force through appropriations, conscriptions of manpower, and other acts of support for the presidential project has also been the subject of debate.[205] Even a lack of congressional disapproval of the military involvement through silence and failure to repudiate the venture have been thought to be a form of congressional consent to the ratification of the President's action. Such a viewpoint is hardly warranted, for it would elevate congressional inaction to the same position as an affirmative delegation or ratification.[206] The invalidity of this view would seem to be borne out by *Greene v. McElroy*,[207] where the Supreme Court was of the opinion that a congressional ratification of certain administrative security programs fixed by the Department of Defense could not be assumed by congressional acquiescence or nonaction. To the contrary, explicit action, "especially in areas of doubtful constitutionality requires careful and purposeful consideration by those responsible for enacting and implementing our laws."[208]

An inference of legislative authorization from appropriations and other support for the military venture through the furnishing of manpower and materials of war has been considered as a mode for the expression of congressional consent. Several intermediate federal court decisions have recognized that authority can be conferred on the President through such acts of support.[209] To satisfy the *Greene* opinion, however, the supporting legislation should identify the presidential action plainly. It should designate or earmark the hostile action being carried on by the President.[210]

Support legislation as authorization for presidential action has, however, been criticized.[211] Assent by Congress should not be gleaned by votes for such legislation, inasmuch as a member of Congress is pressured by a presidential *fait accompli* and must provide for and protect men already called to battle. Thus a vote in the Congress for continued support of the presidential commitment should not be construed as consent to the conflict which is supported. Nevertheless, such supportive legislation was taken to imply consent by a number of lower federal courts, particularly when combined with the Tonkin Resolution. But in *Mitchell v. Laird* two judges repudiated what they called the weight of authority, stating that votes cast by a congressman because "he was unwilling to abandon without support men already fighting" was a compassionate act of aiding those in peril and could not be considered as "proof of consent to the actions that placed them in that dangerous posture."[212] The weight of lower federal court authority, however, reaches an opposite conclusion, and furthermore courts have also held that the form of congressional authorization or participation was a political question because there are no intelligible and objectively manageable standards to gauge the constitutionality of such actions.[213]

7

JUSTICIABILITY

POLITICAL QUESTION

THEORETICAL VIEWPOINTS

THE USE OF FORCE ABROAD by the President without proper congressional authorization or as a transgression of international law may well be considered by the courts to be a political question. It has long been established that the federal judiciary does not decide political questions, for the notion is prevalent that certain matters are entrusted by the Constitution to the political departments of government (that is, to the executive or legislative branches) and thus fall outside of the judicial province. These matters are confided to the political departments alone, and the courts, therefore, will not or should not intervene. This may seem anomalous to one familiar with the principle of judicial review as espoused by Chief Justice John Marshall in the celebrated case of *Marbury v. Madison.*[1] To him the judicial power extends to cases and controversies arising under the Constitution and laws and treaties of the United States.[2] When judicial interpretation and decision of these legal instruments becomes requisite, it behooves the courts to act, not to relinquish their authority. Nevertheless, such abandonment may happen if the question is deemed political, although just what is a political question which calls for judicial abstention rests finally with the courts.[3]

What is a political question? No truly clear-cut definition has emerged which would permit prediction with certainty. The political question doctrine is, according to one writer, "in a state of some confusion."[4] Another has proclaimed that "there is little agreement . . . [as to] its constitutional basis; whether abstention is required or optional; how the courts decide whether a question is political; and which questions are."[5]

In comparing decisions of the Supreme Court in the political question field, one feels that each is *ad hoc* in nature, applicable to that case and state of facts only. Certain theories and explanations, however, do exist as to the meaning of the political question. One explanation asserts that there are gaps or lacunae in the law, and when there are no rules upon which decision can be based, the courts have no power to decide. They are not empowered to create policy.[6] This argument is still resorted to at times in discussing the difference between political and juridical questions in the international legal sphere.[7] But today the assertion is viewed as too simplistic and as based on an out-of-date philosophy which viewed the judges as powerless to formulate law.

A more acceptable rationale views the political question doctrine as a facet of the constitutional principle of the separation of powers. When the Constitution expressly or impliedly commits the sole or exclusive power of decision over a subject matter to a political department of government, it is not within the court's province for determination. If a court did so determine, it would be guilty of usurpation of power, thereby causing a violation of the separation of powers doctrine. This theory permits the judiciary to abstain from decision of a claim only when the power of judicial decision is denied by the Constitution.[8]

Other jurists take a broader viewpoint. It is admitted that courts should abstain constitutionally when the issue has been committed to the autonomous decision of the President or the Congress, but in addition a court might refuse to hear the case for prudential or functional reasons.[9] These reasons permit a certain discretion and flexibility by a court when it is called upon to consider the avoidance of a judicial determination on the merits. Still another approach would allow forbearance on functional grounds. Here the court succumbs to certain practical factors from a judicial point of view, such as problems involved in gaining access to the information or the lack of judicially manageable standards.

Professor Louis Henkin, in researching the political question doctrine, admits that a constitutional commitment for autonomous decision by a political department demands court abstention. Nevertheless, he finds that, for the most part, the political questions cases, particularly in the foreign relations area, are cases in which the court does actually decide the case. Its decision concludes that the conduct of the political department involved was constitutionally within its powers, being neither prohibited nor withheld.[10] In other words, the court decides that the executive or legislative branch was correct in its assessment that this was a political question with which the court could not interfere. As a result it was upheld.

Portions of all of these theories seems to pervade the Supreme Court decisions relating to political questions. In *Baker v. Carr*,[11] Justice Brennan, writing the court's opinion,[12] contended that political question cases were those concerned with "the relationship between the judiciary and the coordinate branches of the Federal Government, and not the judiciary's relation to the states, which gives rise to the 'political question.' "[13] The following listing of factors for consideration in making a determination of a political question was articulated as a test by Justice Brennan:

Prominent on the surface of any case held to involve a political question is found a textually demonstrable constitutional commitment of the issue to a coordinate political department; or a lack of judicially discoverable and manageable standards for resolving it; or the impossibility of deciding without an initial policy determination of a kind clearly for nonjudicial discretion; or the impossibility of a court's undertaking independent resolution without expressing lack of respect due coordinate branches of government; or an unusual need for unquestioning adherence to a political decision already made; or the potentiality of embarrassment from multifarious pronouncements by various departments on one question.[14]

Following this Supreme Court statement, there seem to be three theoretical strands. The first is the constitutional commitment strand, which takes into account the constitutional duty of the courts to decide all cases and controversies arising thereunder unless the Constitution itself grants autonomous determination to a political department not the judicial department. The second two elements (i.e., lack of judicial discoverable and manageable standards or involving the judiciary in nonjudicial policy determinations) of the Brennan test deal with

functional standards and the fundamental approach. The last three factors (a lack of respect for the executive or legislative branch or the
need for complete adherence to an already made political decision or
possibility of conflicting pronouncements on one question) are prudential in character and permit court refusal to pass upon the merits when
not deemed circumspect.[15]

With these criteria in mind, is the use of force abroad by the President without proper congressional authorization, or a use which in-
fringes on international law or on a treaty, a political question which
requires court abstention from decision when cases arise questioning
the legality of the presidential action?

CONSTITUTIONAL COMMITMENT

Baker v. Carr lists as the first element of a political question the
constitutional textual demonstrable commitment to another branch of
government. This mind-boggling, tongue-twisting phrase gives one
pause. We can agree that if the Constitution does in fact give the sole
and autonomous decision over a matter to another department, then the
courts should refrain from interference. To do otherwise would result in
a violation of separation of powers. But the problem as to whether or
not there is such a commitment remains. The Constitution is by no
means clear in declaring when the court may be ousted from all power
of judicial review as a result of a delegation of power to another department.[16] Usually the power is simply granted by the Constitution,
and for the most part the court has little hesitancy in exercising its
judicial authority to decide the case at hand without invoking the political question idea.

Even the most noted authority can reach erroneous conclusions in
finding commitment to a political branch. Professor Herbert Wechsler,
writing before the decision in *Powell v. McCormick*,[17] opined that commitment was explicit as to certain constitutional provisions. He gave
two examples: (1) convictions after impeachment which are given by
Article I, Section 3, solely to the Senate to try, and (2) the seating or
expulsion of members of Congress by each house of the Congress as
permitted by Article I, Section 4 of the Constitution.[18] In *Powell*, the
Supreme Court concluded that there was no constitutional commitment
of autonomous determination to the House of Representatives in its
refusal to seat a member. In reaching this decision the court drew on
language of the Constitution and the intent of its framers, as well as

upon fundamental principles of representative democracy which were believed to be implicit in the Constitution.[19]

Justice Brennan recognized that the question of constitutional commitment is "itself a delicate exercise in constitutional interpretation and is a responsibility of this court as ultimate interpreter of the Constitution."[20] Unfortunately, no Supreme Court interpretation is extant to define clearly the constitutional commitment or lack of it as to presidential use of force abroad without congressional authorization or as violative of international obligations.[21] Authorities have discussed the matter.[22] Many agree that resort to war or sustained hostilities on a large scale and of extensive duration by the President alone should not be undertaken by an autonomous determination by the President, but indeed is or may become an issue for judicial decision.[23] Arguments of justiciability are often based on the bland statement that the Constitution expressly grants to the Congress the power to declare war. Since the power is vested in the legislative, not the executive branch, the judicial power is called upon to decide the constitutional question of separation of powers and prevent unconstitutional usurpations of authority.[24]

Moreover, it is pointed out that the court has decided cases of conflict in the exercise of legislative and executive power as well as the bounds of executive power under the Constitution.[25] The famous case of *Youngstown Steel and Tube Co. v. Sawyer* is cited. The *Steel Seizure* case occurred during the Korean conflict, but the prime issue at hand was not presidential use of force in Korea without congressional authorization. The presidential seizure of the steel mills was occasioned by a domestic labor dispute and a take-over of private property without congressional authorization. The analogy can be made as to separation of powers violation and is apt. Still, the *Steel Seizure Case* can hardly be considered as precedent for presidential use of force abroad. True, the court did see fit to intervene in this allocation of powers issue, and it has seen fit to act in other such instances. On the other hand, examples do exist when the court has adopted a hands-off attitude in such power struggles, for example the amendment of the Constitution as manifested by Article V of the document has been held to grant exclusive power to the Congress over that process.[27] The court has also been consistently of the opinion that the constitutional guarantee of a republican form of government to the states is a political question.[28] In *Goldwater v. Carter*[29] four justices believed that the President's power to terminate a treaty without congressional approval was political in nature. None of these issues is expressly or clearly otherwise committed to a political department.

Turning to that aspect of the political question doctrine which concerns judicial abstention in relation to a violation of international legal obligations, particularly treaties, the United Nations Charter forbids the use of armed force except through collective measures of the organization itself or when exercising the right of individual or collective self-defense.[30] The manner in which hostilities are conducted may be an infringement of the international laws of war, as well as a possible imposition of personal responsibility under the Nuremberg principles. Nuremberg, however, does not seem appropos for consideration here, inasmuch as a lack of personal responsibility for most members of the armed forces through a breach of the Nuremberg rules would for the most part prevent the bringing of a claim; for injury, actual or threatened, necessary to create standing to bring the suit would be lacking.[31]

In a number of cases involving possible infringements of international law and treaties, the courts have seen fit to hear them and have held that the Constitution does not forbid their breach by the President or the Congress. These are cases where the courts have not treated the political question as one requiring abstention for reason of textual commitment or otherwise. To the contrary, the issue has been decided on the merits. The political department is held to have been acting constitutionally in failing to observe the international obligation. Such power over foreign affairs has been granted to the department. Decisions taken by the political department within its constitutional authority have not been considered to be invalid domestically, even though they may be invalid at international law.[32]

The *Prize Cases*,[33] concerning the President's right to institute a belligerent blockade without a congressional declaration of war, illustrate the type of political question in which the court did not abstain from decision, but held the President's independent action to be constitutional.

The action of the First Circuit in the case of *Massachusetts v. Laird*[34] gives some insight into the commitment factor in relation to the presidential deployment of forces in Vietnam. The court had before it the question as to whether the United States involvement in Vietnam was constitutional in the face of a lack of a declaration of war or an explicit ratification by the Congress.

After stating that it would not rely on prudential or functional factors, the court directed its attention to the factor it considered dominant, that is, a textually demonstrable commitment of the issue to a coordinate political department. The court found no express wording emanating from the Constitution to answer the commitment problem, thus a constitutional interpretation involving a construction of the constitutional framework was in order.

In an earlier part of the decision, admission had been made that Congress had the power to declare war independently without presidential cooperation. Moreover, it was noted that the executive could repel attack without the Congress. Beyond these two instances of independent power, the constitutional scheme was thought to envision a joint war-sharing power between the two branches of the government. Furthermore, no answer was given by the Constitution regarding the employment of force to engage in hostilities in the absence of a declaration of war. Nevertheless, it was pointed out that the Founding Fathers understood that hostilities could be conducted in the absence of a declaration of war or in the repelling of a sudden attack. Although the congressional power of declaration might imply a negative that no other branch was empowered to act, the court refused to find a more general negative that without such declaration Congress could not support hostilities beyond repelling an attack. To bolster this position, the court turned to Article I, Section 8, the constitutional power of the Congress to grant letters of marque and reprisal. Such an express grant would not have been necessary if it had been dependent upon a declaration of war only. Thus, the founders must have intended to give Congress the power to authorize hostile action even in time of peace. The old case of *Bas v. Tingy*,[35] which had legitimized a congressionally authorized but undeclared war, and which stated that there could be an enemy even without a declared war, was also cited.

The court then went on to say with respect to the textual commitment problem:

As to the power to conduct undeclared hostilities beyond emergency defense, then, we are inclined to believe that the Constitution in giving some essential power to Congress and others to the Executive, committed the matter to both branches whose joint concord precludes the judiciary from measuring a specific executive action against any specific clause in isolation.[36]

In effect the matter was adjudicated on the merits. The matter of undeclared use of force beyond emergency defense is delegated to both political branches. As long as they share their power in harmony and over a prolonged period, the Constitution has not been breached. This illustrates that type of political question where the court decides, but finds that the Constitution is not violated. The political department or departments are acting within their delegated constitutional powers.

The court did not face the question of instances in which, in the absence of declaration and beyond repelling attack, the two branches were not jointly supportive. "Should either branch be opposed to the continuance of hostilities, however, and present the issue in clear terms, a court might well take a different view."[37]

The latter statement, although a dictum, would lead us to believe that in those instances when the President conducted hostilities without congressional support over a long period of time and in a situation not involving emergency defense, the court might well hear the case and consider such a situation as not presenting a political question.

THE FUNCTIONAL DIMENSION

The second dimension of a political question, according to *Baker v. Carr*, is a functional one, i.e., the lack of judicially discoverable and manageable standards for resolving the issue, as well as the impossibility of deciding without an initial policy of a kind for nonjudicial discretion. It is hard to come to grips with the real meaning of this language. As to the management standards, this factor involves a lack of judicial decisional criteria and relevant data, and possibly the problem of devising effective judicial remedies.[38] Gunther states that this strand "emphasizes the nature of the question and its aptness for judicial resolution in view of judicial competence."[39] For example, in *Coleman v. Miller*,[40] which, among other matters, involved the failure of the passage of the Child Labor Amendment within a reasonable time which caused loss of its vitality, the court stated:

In short, the question of a reasonable time in many cases would involve, as in this case it does involve, an appraisal of a great variety of relevant conditions, political, social and economic, which can hardly be said to be within the appropriate range of evidence receivable in a court of justice and as to which it would be an extravagant extension of judicial authority to assert judicial notice as the basis of deciding a controversay with respect to the validity of an amendment actually ratified.[41]

The court also wondered where criteria were to be found for a judicial determination, for none were found in the Constitution, in a statute, or in the common understanding of the time.

Members of the court often differ as to the existence or non-existence of judicially manageable standards. In *Goldwater v. Carter*, four members held that the issue of presidential termination of a treaty (the defense treaty with Taiwan) without Senate approval was a political question. Noting that the Constitution was silent as to Senate approval in such a case, the court said that different termination procedures may be appropriate for different treaties. This would require that the issue be controlled by political standards. Moreover, since the case involved foreign relations, such relations were largely of a political nature.

Justice Powell disagreed, finding no lack of judicially discoverable and manageable standards. He said: "Resolution of the question may not be easy, but it only requires us to apply normal principles of interpretation to the constitutional provisions at issue."[42]

The initial policy for the nonjudicial discretion element seems to overlap with the lack of judicial manageable standards as well as with some of the prudential elements, for if there is a lack of such standards, or if multifarious pronouncements would cause embarrassment, it would be a matter where the policy decision is left to the political departments. But when is the policy not fit for judicial decision, and just what kind of policy is it that cannot or should not be made by the courts? Justice Douglas indicates, not very helpfully, in a dissenting opinion in *Massachusetts v. Laird*[43] that if the wisdom of the policy is in issue it is not for the courts' determination.[44] The courts often say that they are not concerned with the wisdom of this or that measure with respect to a constitutional interpretation, but this is an easy out which does little to explain, for there is no doubt that courts do make policy decisions, particularly when faced with vague and ambiguous constitutional provisions, and in such decisions one would hope that wisdom plays some part.

The courts have to a large extent regarded foreign relations problems to be policy-making matters within the province of the executive.[45] But even here not all foreign relations issues are regarded as political questions or are viewed as being initial policy outside of judicial cognizance. Justice Brennan speaks of this in *Baker v. Carr*, but again we get little guidance as to which of such foreign relations issues are and which are not political questions. He did conclude in his dissent in *Goldwater v. Carter* that the question of authorization by the Constitution of a branch of government as the repository of power to make a political decision is a constitutional question and that judicially manageable standards would be present.[46] This follows Professor Velvel, who is of the opinion that the question of which branch is the repository of the power to fight a war is a judicial question. He would admit that the decision by the properly designated authority to fight or not to fight could be a political question.[47]

As to the departmental power to commit us to war, he boldly states that the standards are manageable and ordained by the Constitution. This standard he finds in the express wording of the Constitution which grants to the Congress the power to declare war. He would also accept the statements of the Founding Fathers in the constitutional records to the effect that the President may repel sudden attacks without a declaration of war.[48] The actual decision to repel such an attack would be a political question also, but even so the President should not be permitted to continue to fight over a period of time, with as much force as he desires, and at his own discretion and political decision. At some point he must obtain from Congress a declaration of limited or general war.

In *Berk v. Laird*[49] the Second Circuit largely agreed with this thesis. The constitutional grant of power to the Congress to declare war was intended to restrict the President's power to make war on his own initiative. This provision and others in the Constitution placed upon the Congress and the President a duty of mutual participation in the prosecution of military activities abroad over a long duration. The President's conduct of hostilities without significant congressional authorization would be justiciable if the court could determine that it violated a judicially manageable standard as found in Article I, Section 8. The court said:

If the executive branch engaged the nation in prolonged foreign military activities without any significant congressional authorization, a court might be able to determine that this extreme violated a discoverable standard calling for *some* mutual participation by Congress in accordance with Article I, Section 8. But in this case, in which Congress definitely acted, in part expressly through the Gulf of Tonkin Resolution and impliedly through appropriations and other acts in support of the project over a period of years, it is more difficult for Berk to suggest a set of manageable standards and escape the likelihood that his particular claim about this war at this time is a political question.[50]

This opinion tells us straightforwardly that the independent use of force abroad by the President over a prolonged period of time without significant congressional authorization would not be a political question. The congressional grant of power to declare war presents a judicially discoverable and manageable standard. Still, problems do remain.

Both Velvel and the court in *Berk v. Laird* admit that the President does have some independent constitutional power to repel sudden attacks for a limited period of time.[51] International legal rules can be and have been formulated stipulating in general as to what justifies a resort to self-defense. But the rules themselves are vague and subject to dispute by international legal authorities. Courts often decide cases on nebulous rules and conflicting opinions; but their application by a court to decide the constitutionality of a presidential use of force in a claimed exercise of the right of self-defense and without congressional authorization would not be easy. When, for example, is the use of force against attack requisite? Must the attack take place against the actual territory of the attacked state? against its citizens abroad when their lives are endangered and evacuation appears necessary? against its armed forces, its ships, or its planes? against the territory of an allied state in a situation of so-called collective self-defense? Of what magnitude must the attack be to warrant self-defense? How imminent must it be? and how much force is permissible in meeting the attack?[52] If presidential self-defense is justified, how long may its use continue without congressional authorization?[53] These are some of the issues presented for decision, and they seem to be bound up with international political decisions and with those of a military nature. Military and political facts are necessary to resolve them, and such facts and their acquisition are usually not considered to be within the province of the courts. Justice Sutherland in the *Curtiss-Wright* case[54] showed his awareness of this when he noted that the President can know the condition of things in foreign countries better than the Congress can know them, particularly in time of war, for he has diplomatic, consular, and other officials at his command. Sutherland was also of the opinion that if Congress is not well situated to know all the facts, certainly the court is not. Moreover, the effectivity of a judicial remedy is questionable, for a court decision of unconstitutionality might well draw the court into the military and political arena in a way that would necessitate the direction and supervision of the conclusion of the war, a task which a court is hardly equipped to perform. And finally, if the court's decision of unconstitutionality called upon the President to terminate the illegal hostilities, it might bring about presidential defiance of the judiciary. This would not only embarrass and weaken the judicial department, but would also make the court's order ineffective.[55] Judicial criteria, even though not completely lacking, would be sadly deficient. The *Berk* case itself indicates something of the dilemmas when it opines that the drawing of a distinction between offensive and defensive wars would not be easy for the courts.

In *Berk v. Laird*, the Second Circuit was able to find that the initial question of congressional participation in the military venture abroad did not lack a judicially discoverable standard, and that such a standard required mutual participation by the two branches. Left open by the court was the further question as to whether there was sufficient congressional participation through express or implied authorizations or ratifications short of a declaration of war, and whether judicially manageable standards could be formulated to test the adequacy of the congressional authorizations through resolutions, appropriations, raising of armed forces for the hostilities, and other legislative acts of support.

In *Orlando v. Laird*,[56] the court reiterated the *Berk* position that the power to declare war granted to the Congress is a manageable standard which requires mutual executive-legislative participation in the hostilities. Judicial scrutiny could therefore take place as to the existence of mutual participation. The test for such participation was, said the court, "whether there is *any* action by the Congress sufficient to authorize or ratify the military activity in question."[57] This test was met by the Gulf of Tonkin Resolution, congressional appropriations for military operations in Southeast Asia, and the extension of the Selective Service Act with knowledge that inductees under the act would be sent to Vietnam.

As to the form and substance of the congressional authorization, this was held to be a political question. It was a matter of policy constitutionally within the discretion of the Congress and outside the competency of the judicial branch. There were no intelligible and objectively manageable standards which would permit the adjudication of such actions, for they dealt with difficult matters in the field of diplomacy, foreign affairs, and military strategy. "[T]he constitutional propriety of the means by which Congress has chosen to ratify and approve the protracted military operation in Southeast Asia is a political question."[58]

The same court wrestled with the problem again in *Da Costa v. Laird*.[59] Here the legality of the implementation of the President's directive ordering the mining of ports and harbors in North Vietnam and the continuation of air and naval strikes against military targets there was at issue. The crux of the plaintiff's complaint lay in the fact that this unilateral presidential escalation of the war so changed the course of the Vietnam conflict as to make it completely different from that previously authorized and ratified by the Congress, or that such authorization and ratification of the war had been ended by the congressional Mansfield Amendment, which called for the termination of military operations in Vietnam at the earliest possible date. Renewed congressional participation and support had become necessary to make the conflict constitutional. This question of participation, following earlier cases, was not political but judicial.

The district court[60] agreed and came up with a test that would require a determination as to whether the escalation was a foreseeable part of the continued prosecution of the conflict which had been authorized. The Court of Appeals thought that this was an overly simplified viewpoint. It said:

Judges, deficient in military knowledge, lacking vital information upon which to assess the nature of battlefield decisions, and sitting thousands of miles from the field of action, cannot reasonably or appropriately determine whether a specific military operation constitutes an "escalation" of the war or is merely a new tactical approach within a continuing strategic plan. What if, for example, the war "de-escalates" so that it is waged as it was prior to the mining of North Vietnam's harbors, and then "escalates" again? Are the courts required to oversee the conduct of the war on a daily basis, away from the scene of action? In this instance, it was the President's view that the mining of North Vietnam's harbors was necessary to preserve the lives of American soldiers in South Vietnam and to bring the war to a close. History will tell whether or not that assessment was correct, but without the benefit of such extended hindsight we are powerless to know.[61]

Thus an inquiry into the President's domain of tactical and strategic military decisions pursuant to his power as Commander-in-Chief was regarded as a political question.

It was admitted that an escalation of the war might well require additional support by the Congress, and if a manageable standard were presented which would permit judicial resolution, a judicial question would exist. But no such standard had been forthcoming in the case.

This decision was later followed by *Holtzman v. Schlesinger*,[62] where the court had before it the constitutionality of the bombing and other military activities in Cambodia after the removal of American forces and prisoners of war from Vietnam. The District Court issued an injunction prohibiting such military action.[63] A political question was not thought to be involved, for a basic change in the war had occurred through the withdrawal of forces and the repatriation of prisoners. The change now required a judicial determination of congressional participation. Such congressional authority and participation were thought to be a manageable standard. The district judge then found that no authority existed for the Cambodia operation. In the absence of mutual participation by Congress and the President, the bombing and other military action was illegal. In reversing and remanding, the Court of Appeals could see little to distinguish the situation from that presented in the *Da Costa* case. Facts to be determined by the court as to whether the Cambodia bombing brought about a basic change not within the tactical discretion of the President were said to be

precisely the questions of fact involving military and diplomatic expertise not vested in the judiciary, which make the issue political and thus beyond the competency of that court or this court to determine. We are not privy to the information supplied to the Executive by the professional military and diplomatic advisers and even if we were, we are hardly competent to evaluate it. If we were incompetent to judge the significance of the mining and bombing of North Vietnam's harbors and territories, we fail to see our competence to determine that the bombing of Cambodia is a "basic change" in the situation and that it is not a "tactical decision" within the competence of the President.[64]

The decisions of the Court of Appeals in *Da Costa* and *Holtzman* present something of a puzzle. A basic change in the conflict or escalation would require congressional participation through some sort of authorization and would not be a political question. At least the Second Circuit has so suggested. Nevertheless, the court refused to determine whether there had been such a change or escalation, or simply a new tactical approach within a continuing strategic plan. The matter is a political question which must be answered by the military and the diplomats. The court's decision in these two cases relates back to the *Curtiss-Wright* case and the notion that foreign policy and military questions rest within the competency of the executive and the Congress. Their resolve demands a proficiency which the courts do not have, but which does exist in the two political branches and their staffs.

The decisions also suggest that there are institutional checks other than judicial restraint. The Congress can, if it wants to, check the action of the President. If an escalation occurs that is not to the liking of the Congress, it can cut off appropriations; it can institute impeachment proceedings against the President; it can appeal to public opinion through hearings and investigations. Thus court abstention occurs in such an instance where manageable standards are difficult at best to come by.[65]

The courts have not directed their attention to the problem of judicially manageable standards in relation to infringements of international legal obligations by a use of armed force in foreign ventures, whether dealing with resort to force by the state, the method by which the hostilities are conducted, or the potential liabilities of the individual as to his responsibilities in an illegal war. Again these problems would seem to involve that type of political question in which the court does not abstain, but recognizes that the political department is constitutionally empowered to breach the international obligation involved.[66] It might be reasoned, if the issue arose as to whether there was a politcal question demanding court abstention as to a presidential commitment of force abroad in contravention of international obligation, that the problem of a lack of judicially manageable standards would not be insuperable. The judiciary has commonly decided questions of international law and international treaty in controversies which have been brought before the courts by private individuals.[67] International legal rules do exist, and if they prove nebulous, resort to common law principles and methods can be had for decision. But international rules are often vague, conflicting, and subject to dispute. This is particularly true with respect to use of force abroad. What constitutes aggression and intervention is not at all clear. Intervention in time of civil strife is not at all settled. United Nations provisions relating to unilateral use of force and self-defense, individual and collective, are subject to argument, and serious disagreement as to their meaning exists. So much disagreement exists on the international level as to the meaning of many rules that a standards problem could well exist. In attempting to delineate their meaning, a domestic court might well take a different position on an uncertain issue from that taken by other nations.[68]

The situation would not be so difficult in making judicial decisions as to infractions of the laws of war. The United States is a party to a large number of treaties prescribing and proscribing conduct, which should set forth sufficient standards for court determination. Difficulties in obtaining information and facts would not seem to be an insuperable hindrance.

THE PRUDENTIAL DIMENSION

The three prudential factors of *Baker v. Carr* are expressive of the court's desire to avoid a clash with the political branch which is performing the alleged illegal action, in our case a presidential commitment of force abroad without proper congressional authorization. These criteria were almost ignored by the courts in all of their decisions relating to the Vietnam debacle. Legal writers have, however, discussed them. As to the impossibility of independent resolution by the courts without their expressing lack of the respect due coordinate branches of government, one writer belittles this element with a brusque observation to the effect that respect by one department of government by another department of government has hardly been a distinguishing characteristic of the American system.[70] It has also been pointed out that no disrespect is shown to a branch of government when a dispute occurs as to a constitutional interpretation of that branch's powers, for it is the court's duty to be the final arbiter and interpreter of the Constitution, even if its interpretation is not in accord with that of the other department.[71] Justice Douglas notes in his dissent in *Massachusetts v. Laird*: "It is far more important to be respectful of the Constitution than to a coordinate branch of government."[72] Velvel points up the fact that where an interbranch controversy is involved between executive and Congress as to authority to authorize a war, the courts would show respect for Congress and its constitutional power in making a decision of presidential unconstitutionality. No disrespect would be shown to the President, for if it were, then disrespect would have been shown each time the court has struck down a presidential action as outside constitutional bounds.[73] It must be remembered that the court has on occasions addressed itself to the powers of the President vis-à-vis the Congress as well as to his constitutional powers in war and military situations. This criterion seems to be of little importance in a judicial attempt to solve the political question dilemma in matters pertaining to the legality of a presidential use of force abroad.

Is there "an unusual need for unquestioning adherence to a political decision already made"? Some would say that such a factor has no relevance where there is a question of usurpation of constitutional power. This would be particularly true when the matter at issue is concerned with one of the most important decisions a nation might be called on to make, i.e., the problem of peace or war. In such an instance finality should not be given to the presidential decision. To do so would endanger the whole constitutional framework.[74]

Closely related to the need for adherence to a political decision is the final criterion of *Baker v. Carr*, i.e., the potentiality of embarrassment from "multifarious pronouncements by various departments on one question." Just what is signified here by "potentiality of embarrassment"? If it means that embarrassment would result simply because a political branch says that its action is legal and the judiciary disagrees, then the court argues against its function of interpretation of the law and judicial review.[75] Moreover, it has been claimed that any embarrassment which might arise from a judicial decision on the question of the President's power to engage in hostilities abroad is conjectural at best. Such a decision might well be beneficial. The court might decide that the President was so empowered.[76] This would extend a legal aura to his actions and bring about a more wholesome public attitude toward the military action. If the court came out for illegality or unconstitutionality, Congress might then see fit to declare war. This again would probably have a unifying effect on the nation and would elicit a more favorable response from other nations as to the firmness of the United States resolve.[77] If Congress did not see fit to declare war, then efforts toward a peaceful accord would probably be made, and in such an event loss of life and destruction would cease.[78]

On the other hand, the embarrassment and difficulties which might arise from a court pronouncement should not be minimized. Professor Henkin admits that adherence to a political decision already made and the embarrassment which might arise from multifarious pronouncements could well call for court abstention from consideration of

issues of war and peace, or other questions as to which a decision adverse to the political branches could have grave consequences for the national interest, where indeed the President might feel compelled not to heed the Courts. They might refuse, in particular—as in the Viet Nam cases—to step into major confrontation between the President and the Congress to protect the Congressional domain when Congress itself can but will not do it.[79]

It is easy to exaggerate the need for uniformity of decision and the problem of embarrassment from multifarious pronouncements, but dangers do exist when a clash occurs between President and Congress over problems of war and peace. A judicial declaration stating that the United States was acting illegally in resorting to armed force abroad,

whether that illegality was caused by a violation of the Constitution or
of international law or treaty, could have devastating consequences on
the continued conduct of hostilities, orderly withdrawal, and any negotiations for a peaceful end of the conflict. The psychological impact on
the troops and the population of the nation could well be dire. It has
been said that a mere declaratory judgment of illegality should have
little effect on peace negotiations, and, if it did have a negative effect,
the Congress could remedy the problem by a declaration of war.[80] But
what if negotiations did break down? And what if Congress did not
declare war? A judicial declaration of illegality by the Supreme Court
of the United States, whether in the form of a declaratory judgment or
other remedy, would inevitably tend to strengthen the contender and
hinder negotiations for peaceful settlement. And it must always be
remembered that a domestic court decision would be rendered with only
one party to the conflict before the court—the United States.[81]

One finds that similar prudential considerations would tend to make
a court wary in deciding on the merits the question of a violation of
international law by the use of force abroad. To call the hostilities
internationally illegal could hinder peaceful settlement of the conflict in
the same manner as a court declaration of unconstitutionality. The
psychological impact on the contending parties and the nation would
be profound. On the other hand, a court declaration calling certain
conduct violative of the long-established laws of war would not have
such serious consequences. The specific unlawful conduct could be ended.
The continuation of the hostilities between the contenders would be
little affected.[82]

CONCLUSION

Judicial review is such a basic and fundamental principle in the
constitutional system of the United States that shock was felt during
the Vietnam conflict at the refusal of the Supreme Court of the United
States to review the legality of the presidential commitment of armed
forces in the Southeast Asia theater. True, the court did not base its
refusal to review upon the political question doctrine. It either sum-
marily affirmed or denied certiorari of cases coming up to it.[83] Nevertheless, the political question doctrine was invoked in the cases, and the
court's disregard of the problem (other than through certain dissenting
opinions) without a reasoned opinion has been criticized.[84] Even so, a
majority of the court would not introduce itself into what Justice Frank-

furter once called the political thicket.[85] The court in effect capitulated in the Vietnam cases and permitted the decision regarding presidential war-making to be made through the interplay of political forces between the political branches. The court refused to pull political chestnuts out of the fire. In effect, therefore, the matter was up to the Congress, which probably had ample power to have ended the hostilities if it had so desired. The court stayed out of the international political jungle of war and peace.

Lower federal courts were less timorous, but even they approached the issues soft-footedly and with apparent trepidation. As we have seen, the First Circuit in *Massachusetts v. Laird*[86] found a presidential use of armed force abroad, when Congress acquiesces, to be constitutional even though no formal declaration has been made. This is not, however, a political question of the type demanding judicial abstention. This is a political question where the Constitution permits the political departments to act as long as they act in concord.

From other courts of appeals[87] decisions, we know that the constitutional requirement demands joint executive and legislative participation in the initiation of prolonged military activities abroad, and that again this is not a political question. A formal declaration of war is not requisite. Indeed, the form and substance of congressional authorization is a political question.

The cases do not deal with the autonomous power of the President to engage in foreign hostilities other than a recognition of and apparently a restriction of the power to the repelling of sudden attacks.

STANDING AND RIPENESS

Other hurdles which may inhibit judicial review of the issue of the legality of presidential war-making are the requirements of standing and ripeness.[88] If standing is lacking or if the matter which has come before the court is not yet ripe for adjudication, justiciability is lacking and judicial abstention will occur. A decision on the merits is precluded. Standing focuses primarily on the party who seeks to get his complaint before the court and not upon the issues in the dispute. The party must have suffered "some threatened or actual injury resulting from the putatively illegal action and which will be prevented or redressed by the relief sought."[89] Ripeness, on the other hand, is concerned with development of the dispute in a sufficiently specific and concrete manner to permit a court to evaluate the merits of each party's position. It must

not be brought too early or too late.[90] Both standing and ripeness relate
to the case or controversy requirement which is necessary for an exercise
of jurisdiction by federal constitutional courts, but the two are also
bound up with prudential principles which the Supreme Court has
enunciated and which call for judicial self-restraint. When the question
of the legality of a use of force by the President is presented to the
court, the question arises as to whether any of the parties have standing,
and further whether the right asserted is sufficiently developed for court
decision.

The courts have been faced with the problem in cases arising as
a result of the Vietnam conflict. A soldier under orders to report for
duty for the combat to which he objects has been held to have standing to challenge the orders.[91] The orders cause injury and threat thereof,
and there would appear to be a clear-cut causal connection between
that injury and the conduct, i.e., the orders to serve in an allegedly
illegal war.[92] Moreover, the situation could be remedied by the court
through its remedial powers. The dispute seems to be real and not remote
or contingent. Standing was denied, however, to a draft registrant who
refused to submit to induction and who had received no order to report
to the combat area,[93] as well as to one who was simply questioning the
legality of the compulsory selective service law in the absence of a
declaration of war by the Congress.[94]

Again, in *Holzman v. Schlesinger* servicemen plaintiffs were not
permitted to challenge the constitutionality of the Vietnam conflict.
The plaintiffs had been relieved of military obligation, and one had
already been separated from the service. Actually they had been relieved of their combat duties under an Air Force Human Reliability
Program when they sought to question the legality of their orders. The
court held that their appeal for relief was mooted. There was no longer
a case or controversy, for there was no longer continuing harm or significant prospect of harm. The plaintiffs sought to preserve their standing by invoking "the cognizable danger of recurring violation doctrine,"
which would in effect fail to regard an issue as moot if subsequent events
made it clear that the allegedly wrongful conduct could reasonably be
expected to recur. This contention was answered through court reasoning to the effect that the present military status of the plaintiffs, combined with the termination of air strikes in Cambodia, ended any cognizable danger of recurring violation.

Standing was also refused to reservists who claimed that their lives and livelihoods were endangered through a threat of their reactivation because of the use of forces in Cambodia. The United States Court of Appeals in *Mottola v. Nixon*[95] believed that the constitutional guarantee upon which the plaintiffs relied was contingent upon something that might never occur—the reactivization. Neither actual nor threatened injury was alleged. There was only a speculative possibility that the parties would be called upon to serve. No personal stake was present.

Persons and entities other than servicemen and draft registrants have questioned presidential war-making. The Commonwealth of Massachusetts challenged the constitutionality of the Vietnam situation on the basis of an act of its legislature which proscribed military service by its inhabitants in extraterritorial nonemergency armed hostilities without a declaration of war. The court in *Massachusetts v. Laird* noted its doubts as to whether the Commonwealth had proper standing. The court said:

> We do not see, however, that Massachusetts achieves any special status as a protector of the rights of its citizens, and not as a sovereign with unique interests. . . . The traditional rationale is that the federal government is "the ultimate *parens patriae* of every American citizen." . . . This admittedly seems inappropriate in a suit challenging the constitutionality of a war waged by the putative *parens*.[96]

This language, of course, accords with the doctrine of *Massachusetts v. Mellon*,[97] where the Supreme Court held that it was no part of the states' duties to act as *parens patriae* of their citizens in those citizens' relations with the federal government. In such a relationship the United States would represent the citizens. Justice Douglas, in a dissent from a Supreme Court denial of leave to file a complaint in *Massachusetts v. Laird*,[98] complained that the old case of *Massachusetts v. Mellon* did not say that the states could never intervene to protect the rights of their citizens in relation to the federal government. He was of the opinion that the doctrine had been eroded, and further that where the Constitution specifically sets forth the manner in which the federal government must act as *parens patriae* and it fails to do so, then the states may assume the role of *parens patriae* to challenge the federal nonconformity.

Members of the Congress also attacked the constitutionality of the President's use of force in Vietnam. In 1971, thirteen members of the House of Representatives filed a complaint against the President and certain members of the cabinet alleging that for seven years the defendants and their predecessors engaged in war in Indochina without a declaration of war or an explicit congressional authorization for the war. This was an invasion of the constitutional rights of the Congress to make the decision as to whether the United States should fight a war. In *Mitchell v. Laird*,[99] the court of appeals decided that the plaintiffs' reliance upon a breach of duty by the defendants which interfered with plaintiffs' rights as members of Congress to decide upon war did not create standing. To the court, this contention implied an assumption that Congress was exclusively authorized by the Constitution "to decide whether the United States should fight *all* types of war."[100] With this the court disagreed, being of the opinion that there were some types of war which did not need congressional approval, for the President "may respond immediately without such approval to a belligerent attack, or in a grave emergency he may, without congressional approval, take the initiative to wage war."[101] The court did not analyze standing as a legal doctrine, but it did cite Supreme Court cases which have set forth a two-part test for standing. This test requires that the plaintiff must allege injury. Moreover, the interest sought to be protected by the complainant must arguably fall within the zone of interests to be protected or regulated by the statute or constitutional guarantee in question. Here the interest did not, according to the court, fall within the zone of interests protected by the Constitution, for there is no constitutional guarantee that all wars should be initiated by the Congress.

Nevertheless, the court goes on in such a way as to remedy the complaint by an assumption of its own. It assumes that the hostilities which were under way did fall without the constitutional authority of the defendants. If that were true, a declaration by the court "to that effect would bear upon the duties of plaintiffs to consider whether to impeach defendants, and upon plaintiffs' quite distinct and different duties to make appropriations to support the hostilities, or to take other legislative action related to such hostilities, such as raising an army or enacting other civil or criminal legislation."[102] Criticism of the court's reasoning points out that it does not seem to meet the so-called test for standing, which requires a nexus between the action alleged and the injury suffered. This court centered upon a possible future applicability which the judgment might come to possess, rather than upon an injury in fact. This would really amount, in the case under consideration, to a grant of an advisory opinion which is not within the competence of a federal court under Article II of the Constitution.[103]

Holtzman v. Schlesinger[104] involved a single congresswoman who with certain air force officers questioned the constitutionality of the combat operations in Cambodia. The Second Circuit noted that she did not have standing because she, as a member of Congress, had not been denied a right to vote on Cambodia, and further she had engaged in congressional debates on the matter. Representative Holtzman claimed that her votes were ineffective, not because of opposing votes of her colleagues (a majority of the members of the House had voted for an appropriations bill including a provision to end the bombing in Cambodia immediately), but because the bill was vetoed by the President. The court was unimpressed. The fact that the veto was not overridden was due to the contrary votes of her colleagues.

A claim for standing was also made, as in *Mitchell v. Laird*, that a court establishment of illegality could be of import if possible impeachment proceedings were brought against the President. Here the court disagreed with the opinion in the *Mitchell* case on the issue. In firm language it stated:

The claim that the establishment of illegality here would be relevant in possible impeachment proceedings against the President would in effect be asking the judiciary for an advisory opinion which is precisely and historically what the "case and controversy" conditions set forth in Article III, Section 2 of the Constitution forbid. . . . The judgment sought could hardly have any subsequent binding effect on those who have the responsibility for such a measure. Its effect on the named defendants would be clearly academic and moot since they have no interest in controverting it.[105]

The courts have also been faced with the question as to the standing of a citizen and taxpayer to challenge the constitutionality of presidential war-making in the absence of a declaration of war. In the old case of *Massachusetts v. Mellon*, the Supreme Court concluded that a federal taxpayer did not have the power to question the constitutionality of a federal expenditure. The taxpayers' interest was too fluctuating, remote, and infinitesimal. This opinion was modified in *Flast v. Cohen*,[106] where a taxpayer was permitted to challenge a federal expenditure which she claimed would violate the First Amendment's establishment clause. The court set forth a double nexus requirement. The first: a logical link must be established by the taxpayer between the taxpayer's status and the kind of legislation which is attacked. According to the court, to meet this nexus a taxpayer status would be present only when the congressional enactment under the taxing and spending clause of Article I, Section 8 was being attacked. It would not be sufficient to attack an incidental expenditure of tax funds in the administration of what would be primarily a regulatory law. The taxpayer would not have standing if the complaint merely questioned the President's power to engage in undeclared war. Standing as a taxpayer would have to be based on consideration of a congressional appropriation as constitutionally violative of the taxing-spending power. Moreover, in *Velvel v. Nixon*[107] the court was of the opinion that an appropriation for war would be viewed as having been made not under the authority of the taxing and spending power, but under the congressional power to raise and support an army. It might be conceivable, though hardly likely, that the expenditure would be viewed not as based on the taxing and spending clause, but as an incidental administrative expenditure of the Department of Defense.

The second nexus of *Flast* for taxpayer's standing *qua taxpayer* would not seem to be met either. This nexus demands that the taxpayer set forth a nexus between the taxpayer status and the constitutional violation to which the complaint is directed. Specifically it must show an infringement of a limitation imposed under the Constitution upon the congressional power to tax and spend. An attack upon the constitutionality of a use of force by the President does not involve a situation wherein the Congress has contravened a specific constitutional limitation on the spending power. One federal district judge has considered that the congressional power to declare war specifically limits the presidential power, and thus would fall within the meaning of the second nexus in *Flast*.[108] Specific limitations in constitutional law are usually thought of, however, as the "thou shalt nots" or as restrictions upon government, as for example in the Bill of Rights. The power to declare war is an affirmative grant of power to the Congress, not a limitation on the powers of government. Possible usurpation of power by the President might be compared to the usurpation by the Congress of state power alleged in *Massachusetts v. Mellon*. Such an exceeding of congressional power was held in *Flast* not to be within the second nexus.

In *Da Costa v. Laird* the Court of Appeals disagreed with the district court, which had ruled that any citizen "has standing to challenge the validity of action by which large scale international combat or a new departure in belligerency is initiated because the lives of citizens are in mortal danger by such combat."[109] The Court of Appeals refused to accord standing to a generalized interest of all citizens in unconstitutional conduct. This follows Supreme Court doctrine. In *Johnson v. Eisentrager*,[110] the Supreme Court refused standing to a citizen challenging the power of the President to send armed forces abroad. Again in *Schlesinger v. Reservists Committee to Stop the War*,[111] wherein the constitutionality of members of Congress serving in the reserves was questioned as violative of that clause which prohibits persons holding any office of the United States from also being a member of Congress, Chief Justice Burger's majority opinion held that a generalized citizen's interest in constitutionality did not afford access to federal courts. This would be an abstract injury only. Standing would not be precluded, however, just because many people suffer the same injury. Nevertheless, it cannot be claimed if the interest is undifferentiated from that of all other citizens.

SOVEREIGN IMMUNITY

The doctrine of sovereign immunity has been conceived to be a barrier to the jurisdiction of the courts to hear cases where suit has been brought questioning the legality of presidential uses of force without congressional declaration. In *Mitchell v. Laird*, the District of Columbia Circuit Court held that the doctrine of sovereign immunity required dismissal of the case. The sovereign had not consented to be sued. In *Berk v. Laird*, the Second Circuit disagreed, being of the opinion that the doctrine was no bar to the action, and holding that inroads had been made into the doctrine of sovereign immunity. Thus despite the principle, there is no immunity where the action is against an official of the United States government who had no lawful authority to act as he did. A suit against a federal officer will not be dismissed as a suit against the sovereign when the official acts beyond his statutory powers or when his actions transcend the Constitution. A suit against a federal official for alleged unconstitutional conduct in conducting war without congressional declaration or proper authorization should not fall within the principle of sovereign immunity and can be permitted. This was the attitude of the court in *Berk v. Laird*.[112]

8

CONGRESSIONAL ATTEMPTS TO CURB
PRESIDENTIAL POWER

CONGRESSIONAL UNEASINESS over the use of force abroad by American
Presidents has on occasion brought forth legislation attempting to curb
or at least to limit this presidential power. This, of course, gives rise to
the constitutional issue of whether or not this power is subject to legislative control. For those who argue that the President's authority in
these instances is derived directly from the Constitution—from his
powers as Commander-in-Chief, together with his powers over foreign
affairs, to act in self-defense, or faithfully to execute the laws, and
whatever "inherent or residual" powers may be encompassed in the
grant of "executive power" in Article 2—it would seem that it is not
subject to control by Congress. On the other hand, although in the
absence of legislative authorization a President has the authority to
protect American rights and interests abroad by the employment of
force, it is contended that he may not override the provisions of a
duly enacted act of Congress imposing limitations on his right to use
the armed forces beyond the nation's borders. The President's duty to
attend to the faithful execution of the laws of Congress has precedence
over his role as Commander-inChief, his powers over foreign affairs,

116

and the nebulous theories of residual power implied in the words "The executive power shall be vested in the President."[1]

There have been few Supreme Court decisions directly on this point; consequently one must look at extraconstitutional history to resolve this issue, for our system of government developed not only from constitutional interpretation by the court, but also from past precedents and actions of both the executive and legislative branches. Congressional and presidential usage and custom are dynamic elements in constitutional growth.[2]

One of the earliest direct legislative attempts to limit presidential use of force occurred in 1868 when Congress passed a law requiring a President to demand from a foreign government the reason for depriving any American citizen of liberty. If the reply indicated that the American citizen was being wrongfully detained, the President was then to demand the citizen's release. If the foreign government delayed or refused, then the President could use such means, "not amounting to acts of war," as he thought necessary and proper to obtain release.[3] This law was not without its ambiguities. To begin with, it dealt only with the liberty of the person and failed to mention the protection of American property or the possible presidential power of committing forces abroad to pursue a specific foreign policy objective. Did the law mean that Congress sought only to limit the type of action a President could undertake when faced by a situation where an Amreican citizen was illegally deprived of his liberty by a foreign government, leaving the President free to do as he saw fit under his constitutional powers when faced with destruction of American property abroad or in pursuit of some other objective? Or did it mean that Congress intended to deprive all Presidents of the power to commit troops abroad except in the unusual circumstances described by the act? If this latter were true, then what about the understanding at the 1787 Constitutional Convention that the President has the independent power to repel sudden attacks upon the nation, its territories, its ships, its diplomatic missions?[4]

Furthermore, how was a President to interpret his power under the law to take means "not amounting to acts of war"? Acts of war in the broad international law sense of that day and age would not include a wide range of self-help and self-defense measures employing the use of force. Whether or not they would be considered acts of war would depend upon the perception of such actions by the nation at whom they were aimed, and upon that nation's power of retaliation.[5]

In any event, this law did little in the following years to prevent Presidents from ordering the landing of troops to protect American lives and property in Latin America, the Middle East, and the Orient, and certainly never hindered presidential use of dramatic gestures such as the showing of the flag or the sending of the fleet to global trouble spots in pursuance of America's foreign policy. Presidents took many of these actions without seeking direct congressional sanction before or after the fact, and for the most part they were not contested by Congress. Nevertheless, some Presidents, perceiving that a situation might become serious if they sent troops abroad, preferred to do so with approval of Congress for internal as well as international political reasons.[6]

In 1912 Congress again attempted to limit the power of the President to commit troops abroad by tacking a rider to that effect to an appropriations bill. Former Secretary of State Elihu Root, in hearings on the rider, declared that it was within the power of the President to commit troops anywhere in the world, and that the rider would be unconstitutional. So it was dropped.[7]

The Selective Training and Service Act of 1940 included a provision prohibiting the dispatch of American armed forces outside the Western Hemisphere. Yet within a few months of its passage President Franklin Roosevelt sent American troops to Greenland and Iceland without seeking congressional approval.[8]

In spite of numerous incidents where Presidents have in the past deployed armed forces abroad without congressional consent, it was the post–World War II developments which brought to the fore the major debate over the respective spheres of Congress and the President in this particular. The end of World War II found the United States with a large permanent peacetime military establishment, with overseas bases in many parts of the globe, with a widespread network of alliances in the form of collective self-defense treaty commitments under the authority of the United Nations Charter. Furthermore, that instrument banned offensive wars, which may be seen as a limitation on Congress's power to declare war, indicating that offensive wars can no longer be authorized by Congress. Congress theoretically, under the U.N. Charter, can declare only defensive wars based on the inherent right of individual and collective self-defense. But self-defense was interpreted by the constitutional forefathers as a term which permitted the President to act in repelling sudden aggression pursuant to his own independent powers, without going to Congress.[9]

In a number of our collective self-defense treaties, Congress apparently did attempt to control the power of the executive by stating ambiguously that action by each signatory would be taken under the treaties "to meet the common danger in accordance with its constitutional processes."[10] This can be interpreted as preserving to Congress its power to declare defensive war, or, alternatively, it can be said that it in no way took away any power from the executive, since he is constitutionally the Commander-in-Chief and has constitutionally bestowed power in certain instances to use force abroad. As a matter of fact, it can be argued that the phrase may have reinforced if not enlarged the power of the executive; for under his constitutional oath faithfully to execute the laws, he is bound to fulfill our international treaties, which along with the Constitution and laws of Congress are constitutionally designated as the supreme law of the land.

The first major debate over this issue occurred during the Korean conflict, known to many opponents as Truman's war. It was contended that the constitutional processes of the United States required action by Congress as well as by the President before the obligation of the United Nations Charter or any collective defense treaty made thereunder could be translated into action.

When the words "constitutional processes" were incorporated into these mutual defense treaties, it was said that the words were placed there affirmatively to require that the engagement of United States forces in hostilities beyond the emergency authority of the executive should not be undertaken without the specific approval of Congress. Nevertheless, opponents to this position were able to point out that in approving such words to be included in the treaties, the Senate had never precisely spelled out what the correct interpretation of the phrase "constitutional processes" was to be.[11]

Truman continued to base his actions upon his total constitutional powers, including his power as President to enforce our international treaty obligations; and his successors in office, Eisenhower, Kennedy, Johnson, and Nixon, all apparently adopted his stance, sending troops into combat generally prior to either a direct or even an indirect congressional approval.[12]

Nonetheless, as the conflict in Southeast Asia continued month after month, year after year, more and more people began to inquire into the extent of the presidential war-making power. And regardless of the Gulf of Tonkin Resolution and the various appropriations bills which Congress passed to continue the fighting, successive Congresses urged Presidents Johnson and Nixon to bring about peace with honor as quickly as possible. But both seemed to expand the fighting rather than to end it. This brought about a national debate concerning the implementation of governmental foreign policy decisions since World War II. The conventional wisdom passed down through United States history that the conduct of foreign affairs was essentially a presidential prerogative was shaken by this undeclared war that seemed interminable. To those who did not believe that our vital interests required a military presence in Vietnam, it was from its inception an abuse of presidential power. Even those who agreed with the original military involvement became critical of the war's duration and the relative absence of congressional participation in so many major decisions.

In 1967, a Senate committee began to hold hearings on a "National Commitments Resolution." That committee affirmed that the members thereof did "not believe that formal declarations of war are the only available means by which Congress can authorize the President to initiate limited or general hostilities. Joint Resolutions such as those pertaining to Formosa, the Middle East and the Gulf of Tonkin are a proper method for granting authority."[13]

In June, 1969, the Senate did pass the "National Commitments Resolution." The measure declared that the pledge or actual use of U.S. armed forces outside the United States should result *only* from joint action taken by the legislative and executive branches by means of a treaty, statute, or concurrent resolution of both houses specifically providing for such commitment. This resolution was simply a "sense of the Senate" resolution without force of law. It did not nullify previously wide-ranging executive agreements and defense treaties.

Another approach seeking reassertion of congressional prerogative involved the introduction of numerous bills and resolutions which would have cut off funds for Southeast Asian operations in order to achieve a total United States withdrawal from Vietnam. But Congress continued to appropriate money to support the Southeast Asian operations, implicitly acknowledging that once American troops were committed in war, Congress had little choice but to support them. The power to cut off appropriations seemed too drastic to be used as an effective tool to circumscribe presidential power.[14]

In December, 1969, Congress did enact a measure seeking to limit the extension of the war. The measure barred the introduction of ground combat troops into Thailand and Laos. The administration ultimately endorsed the measure.[15]

Early in 1970, the House conceded certain war-making prerogatives to the President in the House War Powers Resolution, passed by a vote of 289 to 39. It recognized that in certain extraordinary and emergency circumstances the President had the authority to defend the United States and its citizens without specific prior authorization by Congress. Instead of trying to define the precise conditions under which Presidents might act, the House relied on procedural safeguards. The President would be required "whenever feasible" to consult with Congress before sending American forces into armed conflict. He was also to report the circumstances necessitating the action, the constitutional, legislative, and treaty provisions authorizing the action, together with his reasons for not seeking specific prior congressional authorization; and he was to include the estimated scope of activities.[16] The Senate did not act on the measure. Because of mounting national frustration with the war, early in 1970 President Nixon announced his plan for the Vietnamization of the struggle and established a timetable for withdrawal of American troops. But he shattered his credibility when in April, 1970, he decided to send American troops into Cambodia on his own authority, without congressional consultation or authorization. He announced that the purpose of the mission was to clean out communist border sanctuaries for the Vietcong and North Vietnamese, and that the operation was a limited one, to last only two months, until June 30. He defended his decision in terms of a strategical maneuver to protect the safety of American armed forces still in Vietnam. Cambodian inability to control these sanctuaries "clearly endangered the lives of Americans who are in Vietnam now and would constitute an unacceptable risk to those who will be there after withdrawal of another 150,000."[17]

The decision to send troops abroad can presumably be distinguished from how the troops will be used after combat has started. In most cases, the conduct of the war is considered to be the exclusive province of the President as Commander-in-Chief. Thus it was the Nixon thesis that sending these troops into Cambodia was merely a combat decision made during the course of an already existing armed conflict. As defended by William H. Rehnquist, then assistant attorney general for the Office of Legal Counsel of the Department of Justice, the President's authorization of the Cambodian cleanup was "precisely the sort of tactical decision traditionally confined to the Commander-in-Chief in the conduct of armed conflict."[18] It was, Rehnquist said, a decision made during the existence of an armed conflict on how that conflict should be carried on, rather than a determination that some new and previously unauthorized military venture should be undertaken.

To many Americans, this appeared to be a reversal of previous presidential pledges to end "with honor" American involvement in Southeast Asia. Nixon had acted on the conviction that the responsibility for this decision was his alone. Nevertheless, it was the opinion of many congressmen that the implications of such a step as the invasion of Cambodia, even for a short period of time, were so profound that no President should be permitted to initiate such an important move without congressional consultation. These members of Congress felt that it was an escalation of presidential powers inconsistent with the Constitution's grant to Congress to declare war. They viewed the Commander-in-Chief role as limited to the conduct of the war and management of operations, which did not embrace the power to broaden the scope of hostilities by invading yet another nation.

The Constitution grants to Congress not only the power to declare war, but also the power to raise, support, and regulate the military forces; but it does not give to Congress the power of tactical and military strategy, which correctly belongs to the Commander-in-Chief role. But, as seen in the Cambodian situation, the dividing line between the powers of one and the powers of the other can indeed be nebulous.

The Senate began immediate debate on measures that could be taken to bring about a more nearly equal balance between the executive and legislative branches in making and undertaking foreign military commitments. The vehicle for the Senate discussion was an amendment to a bill extending for two years the Foreign Military Sales Act of 1968. The amendment, sponsored by Senator John Sherman Cooper and Senator Frank Church, sought to prohibit funds from being expanded to retain U.S. combat forces or advisers in Cambodia after July 1, 1970, without specific congressional approval. It did not bar air activity over Cambodia. Although the Cooper-Church Amendment was accepted by the Senate, its meaning and actual effect were cast in doubt by a series of amendments which reaffirmed the President's constitutional powers, including his right to take whatever action was necessary to protect the lives of United States armed forces wherever deployed. The Cooper-Church Amendment passed the Senate just as the last of the United

States troops were being pulled out of Cambodia in accordance with President Nixon's pledge that the operation to clean out communist border sanctuaries would be complete by June 30.[19] On July 9 the House rejected the Cooper-Church Amendment.[20] Thereupon, the following day the Senate passed a concurrent resolution repealing the Gulf of Tonkin Resolution.[21] This repeal was added as a rider to the Foreign Military Sales Act.

House Minority Leader Gerald R. Ford stated that the Nixon administration would not object to the House's concurring in this rider, since the Gulf of Tonkin Resolution had become "obsolete."[22] He declared that the authority for military action in Southeast Asia derived from the President's constitutional prerogatives and obligations as Commander-in-Chief. On July 1, 1970, in a televised interview, when questioned by newsmen on the legal justification for continuing to fight an undeclared war in Vietnam if the Gulf of Tonkin Resolution were repealed, Nixon responded that the President "has the constitutional right, not only the right but the responsibility to use his powers to protect American forces when they are engaged in military actions."[23] When, on January 1, 1971, the Foreign Military Sales Act of 1971[24] with its Gulf of Tonkin repeal rider was finally presented to Nixon for his signature, he again reaffirmed that he did not need the authority of the resolution "to wind down the war," since that power was contained within his Commander-in-Chief powers.[25]

In repealing the Gulf of Tonkin Resolution, the Congress still left the SEATO treaty untouched. Among other things, the American entry into the Vietnam conflict was based in part on this treaty. As Truman stated, in the Korean war one of his bases for action was his authority as President to ensure that the treaties of the United States (specifically in the Korean case the United Nations Charter) be faithfully executed as supreme law of the land.[26] If Truman's view of the matter be accepted, nothing much was changed in the Vietnam situation by the repeal of the Tonkin Resolution, because the President could still use the SEATO Treaty as one of his legitimate bases for continuing military operations.

Initially brought up during the Senate debate on the Cooper-Church Amendment was another amendment known as the Hatfield-McGovern "end the war" amendment. This would have limited U.S. troop strength in Vietnam to 280,000 men by April 30, 1971 (close to 284,000 projected a few months earlier by President Nixon). The amendment would have limited the use of funds after that date to financing the complete withdrawal of all remaining troops by December 31, 1971, although it did authorize the President to extend the withdrawal date for a period not to exceed sixty days in case of a clear and present danger to U.S. troops. But this amendment was rejected by a majority of the Senate because the North Vietnamese held many American prisoners of war, and the fate of these prisoners would be at the mercy of the North Vietnamese if the bargaining pressure of the United States were loosened by an absolute deadline for troop removal.[27]

Congressional opponents of the Vietnam War tried throughout 1971 to assert the powers of Congress to force an early end to the role of the United States in Southeast Asia. Three times the Senate approved amendments sponsored by Majority Leader Mike Mansfield to various legislative enactments, declaring United States policy to be the withdrawal of all American troops from the area by a certain date. The first version was attached to a bill extending the draft; the second to a defense procurement bill; and the third to a foreign aid authorization bill. The first version set the withdrawal deadline at nine months after enactment of the measure, while the other two allowed six months for withdrawal. All three amendments made withdrawal contingent upon the release of American prisoners of war, held by the North Vietnamese and the Viet Cong. All three amendments also urged the President to set a final date for withdrawal within the specific time frame, and to negotiate with the North Vietnamese for an immediate cease-fire and for a series of phased withdrawals of United States troops in exchange for a series of phased releases of American prisoners, to be completed by the date set by the President, but no later than the deadlines specified.[28]

The House, in action on the Mansfield amendment to the draft extension bill, modified the amendment by deleting the deadline and adding language declaring that it was the sense of Congress that the United States should terminate military operations in Southeast Asia "at the earliest practicable date." After long debate this language was accepted by the Senate, and the President signed it into law.[29] In action on the Mansfield amendment to the defense procurement bill, the House again insisted that the wording be modified to remove the withdrawal deadline and replace it with the language "at a date certain," a modification again accepted reluctantly by the Senate. In signing the defense procurement bill, President Nixon declared that in his opinion the amendment was "without binding force or effect."[30] The House stalled final action on the third Mansfield amendment to the foreign aid bill until the 92nd Congress ended its first session. When the foreign aid bill was passed by the House during the second session, the Mansfield amendment was omitted, an action which was reluctantly accepted by the Senate.[31]

In 1972, the Senate again sought to place restrictions on the President's use of force without prior congressional approval by passing the Senate War Powers Bill. In February, 1972, the Senate Foreign Relations Committee reported that a strict interpretation of the constitutional clause giving Congress the right to make all laws "necessary and proper" for carrying into execution its constitutional grants of powers to declare war and raise and support armies permitted Congress to define and codify the powers of the government, including those of the President in decisions involving the United States in hostilities, such as future Vietnams.[32] The Senate bill, which was passed in April, 1972,[33] provided that in the absence of a declaration of war by Congress, armed forces could be committed to hostilities, or to situations where imminent involvement in hostilities is clearly indicated by the circumstances, only to repel an armed attack on the United States or to forestall the direct and imminent threat of such an attack; to repel an armed attack against United States armed forces outside the United States or to forestall the threat of such attack; or to protect and evacuate United States citizens and nationals in another country if their lives were threatened, pursuant to specific statutory authorization by Congress, not to be inferred by any existing or future law or treaty unless specific authorization was provided. Specific statutory authority would also be required for the assignment of United States military personnel to assist a foreign nation's forces in hostilities or a situation where hostilities were imminent. The bill allowed the President to take armed action to protect United States citizens and nationals on the high seas. It assured continued participation by United States officers in joint military commands, such as NATO, with other nations. It allowed the President to use the armed forces if necessary to protect U.S. forces as they withdrew from hostilities, if Congress refused to authorize their continued use after thirty days, or if an attack on the United States prevented Congress from meeting before the thirty-day deadline expired on presidential action not authorized by Congress. It required the President to report promptly to the Congress the commitment of forces for any of the purposes above. And it limited to thirty days the length of involvement of United States forces unless Congress by specific legislation authorized their continued use. It provided that Congress by act or joint resolution could terminate the use of United States forces by the President before the end of the thirty-day period. And it set procedures to require prompt consideration in both houses of any bill or joint resolution authorizing or terminating the use of American forces committed by the President. It specifically exempted the ongoing Indochina war from its provisions.[34]

This bill was strongly opposed by the Nixon administration, which successfully lobbied for its defeat in the House, which passed a much more modified version of the Senate War Powers Bill. The House version dropped the Senate requirements. It merely urged the President to consult with Congress before sending Americans into armed conflict.[35] House and Senate committee conferees could make no headway in resolving the differences between the two bills, and the bills died at the end of the congressional session.

Early in December, 1972, President Nixon suspended peace negotiations which were being carried on in Paris seeking to end the war in Southeast Asia, and again resumed heavy bombing in North Vietnam, in spite of many doubts entertained by leading congressmen on this action.[36] Secretary of State Henry Kissinger returned to the bargaining table late in December; and on January 27, 1973,[37] the longest war in United States history began to draw to a close with the signing of the peace agreement between the United States, South Vietnam, North Vietnam, and the Viet Cong. Implementation of the agreement was not without setbacks and threats of disintegration. There were several impasses over the timetable for releasing the prisoners of war; but finally, on March 29, 1973,[38] the last known prisoners held by the North Vietnamese were released, and the United States withdrew its remaining 2,500 troops from South Vietnam. With the termination of direct U.S. military involvement in Vietnam, and the signing of a cease-fire in Laos February 21, 1973,[39] attention shifted to the continuing war in neighboring Cambodia.

The 93rd Congress convened in January, 1973, in a defiant mood. Both the House and Senate Democrats (in the majority) meeting in caucus passed resolutions calling for an end to all monetary appropriations used to continue American participation in Southeast Asia once the prisoners of war were returned. And the President's decision to keep up heavy U.S. bombing over Cambodia sparked the beginning of the 1973 challenge by Congress to the presidential war-making powers, as members questioned Nixon's constitutional authority to continue the bombing without obtaining explicit congressional authorization.

The congressional movement to cut off the bombing gathered momentum early in May. The test of congressional sentiment came during consideration of an amendment to a second supplemental appropriations[40] bill prohibiting the Defense Department from transferring $430 million from other defense programs to fund further United States military activity in or over Cambodia. The Senate followed suit, and on June 26 the Congress sent the bill to the White House, where it was promptly vetoed by Nixon.[41] But the democratically controlled Congress warned Nixon that the prohibition would be added to all other bills. So on June 29 Nixon agreed to a compromise solution that would allow him to continue the bombing for another few weeks while negotiations to reach a cease-fire in Cambodia were carried on. Thereupon the House passed a second supplemental appropriations bill that barred the use of any previously appropriated funds to support American combat activities in or over Cambodia and Laos after August 15.[42] Minority Leader Gerald Ford assured the House that he had been in contact with Nixon, who had assured him that the President would either stop the bombing by August 15 or seek specific approval from Congress to continue combat activities.[43] The Senate also passed this bill on June 29, clearing the bill for the President, who signed it into law on July 1.[44] This was the first action ever taken by Congress to stop United States military involvement in the Indochina war.

As has been seen, an attempt to persuade the courts to cut off the Cambodian bombing prior to August 15 failed. On July 25, a New York federal district court judge had issued a permanent injunction immediately barring all further United States military actions in Cambodia because the bombing was unconstitutional, as there had been "no congressional authorization to fight in Cambodia after the withdrawal of American troops and the release of American prisoners of war." On July 27, upon appeal by the government to the Second Circuit Court of Appeals, the effective date of the order was delayed by the appellate court, which agreed to hear arguments on the order on August 8. But on August 4, Justice William Douglas of the Supreme Court reinstated the New York Federal Court's halting of the bombing, on the grounds that this was a capital case involving life and death, and when a request for a stay in a capital case is before any judge of the Supreme Court, the stay must be granted because death is inevitable. He carefully stated he was not sitting on the merits of the case; that is, he was not making any decision as to whether or not the bombing of Cambodia was constitutional. With the law's deadline but eleven days off, the full Supreme Court met in emergency session and reversed the Douglas ruling.[45]

Both the House and the Senate were now determined to assume more responsibility for future decisions on whether the United States should engage in armed conflict, and the two houses began to debate a joint resolution known as the War Powers Resolution. The original House version did not attempt to define or codify presidential war powers. It directed the President "in every possible instance" to consult with Congress before introducing forces into hostilities or situations where hostilities might be imminent. If unable to do so, he was to report to Congress within 72 hours, setting forth the circumstances and details of his action. Unless Congress declared war within 120 days or specifically authorized the use of force, the President had to terminate the commitment and remove the troops. Congress could also direct disengagement any time during the 120-day period by passing a concurrent resolution, a measure that would not require the President's signature and, therefore, would avoid the possibility of a veto.[46]

Opponents of the bill objected to the concurrent resolution provision, as well as the automatic termination of a commitment at the end of 120 days unless Congress acted to extend it. House Republican Leader Gerald Ford declared that congressmen "should have the guts and the will to stand up and vote 'against the commitment of forces abroad' instead of saying 'you cannot do it' by doing nothing."[47]

The Senate attempted to spell out the conditions under which Presidents could take unilateral action. Armed force could be used in three situations: (1) to repel an armed attack upon the United States, its territories and possessions, to retaliate in the event of such an attack, and to forestall the direct and imminent threat of such an attack; (2) to repel an armed attack against United States armed forces located outside the United States and its territories and possessions, and to forestall the direct and imminent threat of such an attack; and (3) to rescue endangered American citizens and nationals in foreign countries or at sea.

The first situation, except for the final clause, probably conforms to the understanding developed at the Constitutional Convention in Philadelphia. The other situations reflect the changes that have occurred in the concept of defensive war and life and property actions. The Senate bill required the President to cease military action unless Congress within thirty days specifically authorized the President to continue. A separate provision allowed him to sustain military operations beyond the thirty-day limit if he determined that "unavoidable military necessity" respecting the safety of the armed forces required their continued use for the purposes "of bringing about a prompt disengagement."[48]

Under the Senate version, Congress could end United States involvement before the expiration of the thirty-day period by a bill or joint resolution, either of which could be vetoed by the President. Senators opposing the bill were confident of a presidential veto if the measure reached the White House, so they did not mount a serious challenge to the Senate version.

The bill was then sent to a joint House-Senate conference committee. The Senate's delineation of circumstances under which the President could commit United States troops abroad without a declaration of war proved to be the major stumbling block in the conference. The Senate version would have stated in operative terms, rather than merely as the understanding of Congress, the circumstances in which the armed forces may be introduced into hostilities without a declaration of war. The Senate version also differed from the House version in two other important respects. It would have explicitly allowed the President to introduce the armed forces to evacuate United States citizens and nationals abroad in certain emergency situations, and, by avoiding reference to the Constitution in defining the circumstances in which the President could independently engage the armed forces in hostilities, it would have avoided indicating that the President does have a constitutional right to act on his own in certain circumstances.

The Senate conferees made key concessions to the House on this provision, accepting a general policy statement that in the absence of a declaration of war or specific statutory authorization, the President could commit troops only in response to "a national emergency created by attack upon the United States, its territories or possessions, or its armed forces."

Conferees settled on a 60-day deadline on commitment of U.S. troops abroad unless Congress (1) declared war; (2) specifically authorized its continuation; or (3) was unable to meet in session as a result of an armed attack upon the United States. Both the House and Senate versions had included definite deadlines on troop commitment, the House 120 days, the Senate 30 days. The 60-day period could be extended under the conference version for up to 30 days to provide for the safe withdrawal of U.S. troops. A similar provision had been included in the Senate bill, but without the 30-day limitation.

The controversial "concurrent resolution" to terminate any commitment of troops abroad that was part of the House version was incorporated without change in the conference compromise. The House and Senate versions had contained similar reporting requirements. In conference, a 48-hour deadline was set for an initial presidential report on his deployment of United States forces. The House resolution had called for the President to report in writing within 72 hours, while the Senate had called for the action to be reported "promptly." Both versions called for follow-up consultation between the White House and Congress. The Senate language requiring a report at least once every six months during continuing American involvement was incorporated in the conference version. Conferees also agreed to House provisions relating to the transmittal of the presidential report to Congress, but added amendments authorizing the reconvening of Congress, in the event that it was not in session, to receive the report.[49]

The compromise measure, which was then passed by both houses on October 10, 1973, was sent to the President for signature.[50] President Nixon promptly vetoed it. He stated in his veto message that the War Powers Resolution was an attempt to take away by a mere legislative act authorities which the President had properly exercised under the Constitution for almost two hundred years. He declared:

One of its provisions would automatically cut off certain authorities after 60 days unless Congress extended them. Another would allow the Congress to eliminate certain authorities merely by the passage of a concurrent resolution—an action which does not normally have the force of law, since it denies the President his constitutional role in approving legislation. I believe that both these provisions are unconstitutional.

He reminded Congress that the "only way in which the constitutional powers of a branch of the government can be altered is by amending the Constitution—and any attempt to make such alterations by legislation alone is clearly without force."[51]

The War Powers Resolution of 1973 was then repassed by two thirds of the House and Senate over the President's veto.[52] Some of the congressional support for overriding the veto was based on party politics and symbolic value rather than on the resolution's contents. For example, a number of members of the House had voted against the original House bill and against the final version which came out of the joint conference committee, and yet voted to override the veto. Some did so because they felt that failure to vote to override the veto would mean that they supported the arguments advanced by Nixon in his veto message. Others did so because eight times during the 93rd Congress Nixon had vetoed legislation and Congress had failed to override those vetoes, and they looked upon overriding this veto as a way to reassert the power of Congress in the field of legislation.

The War Powers Resolution sets forth three main procedures: (1) Presidential consultation with Congress; (2) Presidential reports to Congress; and (3) Congressional termination of military action. The purpose of the Resolution, according to Section 2(a), is to "fulfill the intention of the framers of the Constitution . . . and insure that the collective judgment of both Congress and the President will apply" to the deployment of troops abroad. When the members of Congress solemnly affirm that they are fulfilling "the intent of the framers of the Constitution," they are invoking a sacred formula which has much sound and fury but little substance. Some of the fifty-five men who attended the Constitutional Convention during that long hot summer of 1787 spoke very little; some did not attend all of the sessions, for the Convention lasted from May 25 until September 15, and some had to return home periodically to attend to their affairs. Even though others may have participated in the debates, eventually only forty signed the final version of the document. Since the document had to be ratified by the people of the various states in specially called conventions, they too can be considered "framers," yet little is recorded of their debates or "intent."[53] Application of "the intention of the framers" to foreign policy decisions in the last quarter of the twentieth century is reminiscent of the old comic routine:: "Does your sister like candy?" "I don't have a sister." "If you had a sister would she like candy?" And the phrase "to insure the collective judgment," if examined in the light of other sections of the resolution, together with executive interpretations and congressional behavior since its passage, supplies evidence that collective judgment is by no means assured.

This collective judgment is to apply whenever the President seeks "the introduction of United States Armed forces into hostilities or into situations where imminent involvement in hostilities is clearly indicated by the circumstances." This phrase is not free from ambiguity. Hostilities have varied in their significance as well as their magnitude. They can run a whole spectrum of activities from minor breaches of the peace to major international wars.

The presidential aggregate of constitutional powers has generally permitted a President to dispatch troops, ships, and planes abroad in peacetime in response to international events with the hope that such deployment will prevent hostilities or "imminent involvement." There is no single pattern of engagement of armed forces in hostilities. If congressional collaboration is required whenever any deployment of military forces is required, Presidents may feel that the Joint Resolution violates their constitutional mandates and hence may ignore the law's restrictions. In this way the War Powers Resolution can become the vehicle for expanding rather than a means for restricting presidential power.

In addition, Presidents in the future may well argue at the time of deployment of troops abroad there was no "clear" indication that they might be "imminently" involved in hostilities. Dispatching of troops is not the only way to provoke hostilities. History is replete with instances where the enforcement or denunciation of a treaty, or the severance of diplomatic relations, has led to hostilities.

Section 2(c) seems to presume that the President must generally seek congressional approval to deploy American forces abroad, except in a few emergency instances where presidential initiative is retained. The presumption runs in favor of Congress, according to Section 2(b), because of the "necessary and proper" clause which gives Congress the power to make all laws necessary and proper for carrying into execution all other powers vested by the Constitution in the government or in an officer of the United States. Despite this statement, there still remains unanswered the question of whether or not there do remain under the Constitution exclusive executive powers which cannot be subjected to congressional conditions.

Some have taken the position that as the authority of the President to employ armed forces is derived directly from the Constitution, it is not subject to congressional control. This view is supported by language in *Durand v. Hollins* wherein Justice Nelson, in speaking of presidential discretion to use force abroad, categorically affirmed that "there exists, and can exist, no power to control that discretion."[54] Others say that in the absence of legislative authorization the President may employ armed forces abroad to protect American rights and interests, but that he cannot override a duly enacted act of Congress, since he is by oath bound to attend to the "faithful execution" of the laws.[55]

Section 2(c) of the resolution seems to restrict presidential power by claiming that the constitutional powers of the President as Commander-in-Chief to deploy forces abroad is limited to three types of situations: (1) a declaration of war, (2) specific statutory authorization, or (3) a national emergency created by "attack upon the United States, its territories, or possessions, or its armed forces."

If these were the outer constitutional limits of the presidential deployment of forces power, then, for example, President Kennedy acted beyond his powers during the Cuban missile crisis, for in that case there had not been an attack upon the United States, its territories or possessions, or its armed forces. As a matter of fact, the warheads were not yet on the missiles, and the naval forces were dispatched mainly to preserve the balance of power in the Western Hemisphere.[56]

This section of the resolution, in speaking to the presidential powers as Commander-in-Chief, does not take into consideration the powers of the President to execute as supreme law of the land the treaties of the United States, using the inherent right of individual and collective self-defense under the United Nations Charter and other collective security treaties, nor does it speak to his power as the sole voice of the nation in foreign affairs, or to those inherent powers residual in the term "executive power." So future Presidents could presumably bypass the resolution by claiming they are acting under other constitutional grants than that to the Commander-in-Chief.

This was the basis of the argument of Monroe Leigh, legal adviser to the State Department and spokesman for the Ford administration. He cited other situations in which the President had constitutional authority to introduce armed forces into hostilities such as (1) to rescue American citizen abroad; (2) to rescue foreign nationals where such action directly facilitates the rescue of American citizens abroad; (3) to protect American embassies and legations abroad; (4) to suppress civil insurrection; (5) to implement and administer the terms of an armistice or cease-fire designated to terminate hostilities involving the United States; and (6) to carry out the terms of security commitments contained in our treaties. He added, "We do not, however, believe that any such list can be a complete one, just as we do not believe that any single definitional statement can clearly encompass every conceivable situation in which the President's Commander-in-Chief authority could be exercised."[57] In other words, Leigh was of the opinion not only that the President could invoke other of his constitutional powers, but that the attempted congressional definition of Commander-in-Chief powers was incomplete.

The first procedure to insure "the collective judgment" called for in Section 2(a) is the requirement that the President shall "in every possible instance" consult "with Congress before introducing United States armed forces into hostilities or into situations where imminent involvement in hostilities is clearly indicated." The language "in every possible instance" obviously leaves considerable discretion to the President as to the form and times of consultation. The Carter administration noted that the President's responsibilities under the sections involving consultation and reporting "have not been delegated, so that the final decision as to whether consultation is possible and as to the manner in which consultation be undertaken or reports submitted rests with the President."[58] In other words, the President has the power to determine that a particular decision to commit forces abroad is not a "possible instance" to consult with Congress.

Does the resolution mean that the President must consult with all 535 legislators? If so, it would be an impossible task, if the word "consult" means more than "to inform." As Congress has not organized a specific body with whom the President is to consult—assuming "consult" means to exchange observations and views—does that mean the President may choose and select those with whom he wishes to consult? For example, would the Speaker of the House and the President of the Senate be sufficient? Or should it be the leadership of both parties in both houses? Or the chairman and ranking members of designated committees? The problem here is that even if the President should consult with certain ranking members of the House and Senate, their approval of his proposed actions would by no means insure that a majority of both houses or of either house would agree. Furthermore, as Congress as a whole is not and can never be privy to all the information available to the President in time of emergency, seeking congressional advice could turn into an exercise in futility. This President Ford pointed out after he had retired from the presidency, stating that "there is absolutely no way American foreign policy can be conducted or military operations commanded by 535 members of Congress even if they all happened to be on Capitol Hill when they are needed."[59]

Section 2(c) does seem to concede that the President as Commander-in-Chief has some inherent constitutional power to introduce armed forces into hostilities on his own authority. But this may be weakened by Section 5(c), which is referred to by many as the "congressional veto." This section states "at any time that United States Armed Forces are engaged in hostilities outside the territory of the United States, its possessions and territories without a declaration of war or specific statutory authorization, such forces shall be removed by the President if the Congress so directs by concurrent resolution."

Congress began to incorporate this type of concurrent resolution veto device in legislation as far back as 1933. Since then there has been controversy over its constitutionality. Its legality may vary according to the type of legislation involved. There has been no definite ruling by the Supreme Court on this issue, so one can merely speculate as to its validity in the present context. But it would seem that here it would be of questionable constitutionality. As the legal adviser of the Department of State pointed out: "if the President has the power to put men there in the first place, that power could not be taken away by concurrent resolution because the power is constitutional in nature."[60]

Every President as far back as Franklin Roosevelt has opposed legislative veto provisions that encroach upon the power of the executive. And on March 8, 1981, Attorney General William French Smith, as spokesman for President Reagan, declared that he would seek to obtain in the future a decision from the Supreme Court declaring certain legislative vetoes to be unconstitutional if they intruded upon the President's constitutional powers. "As a general proposition, we view a legislative veto that intrudes on the authority of the President as being unconstitutional."[61]

Over and above consultation, Section 4(a) requires that the President shall report in writing within forty-eight hours to the Speaker of the House and the President Pro Tempore of the Senate, not only on his deployment of troops "into hostilities or into situations where imminent involvement in hostilities is clearly indicated by the circumstances," but also when armed forces are introduced into the territory, airspace, or waters of a foreign nation, while equipped for combat or in numbers which substantially enlarge United States armed forces equipped for combat already located in a foreign nation. Again there is a lack of clarity here. In the first place, since World War II there has been absolutely no international legal consensus on how far up the "airspace" of a nation extends; nor has there been universal acceptance of how far out the territorial waters of a nation extend.

Does this language take away from Presidents the long-used right of showing the flag in various areas of the world? For example, would sending additional ships to the Persian Gulf or the Indian Ocean require such a report? Or is the new "rapid deployment force" being sent abroad a new commitment requiring report, or a "substantial enlargement" equally requiring a report?

In any event, when the President does submit a report, this report is to be referred immediately to the House Committee on Foreign Affairs and the Senate Committee on Foreign Relations. Thereafter, within sixty days, unless Congress has declared war, or enacted a specific authorization for such use of United States armed forces, or extended by law the sixty-day period, or is physically unable to meet as a result of an armed attack upon the United States, the President may extend the sixty-day period by an additional thirty days if he determines that force is needed to protect the removal of American troops. Congress has two means of control, either a decision not to support the President during the sixty-to-ninety day period, or passage of a concurrent resolution at any time to direct the President to remove the forces engaged in hostilities.

The conference report on the Joint Resolution explained that the sections on consultation, reporting, and congressional action are not dependent upon the restrictive language of Section 2(c).[62] Consequently it would seem that in many instances the President could use his own judgment as to when and where to introduce forces into hostilities. He could so firmly commit the nation's forces and prestige during the sixty-to-ninety-day period that Congress would find it politically and militarily impossible to reverse the operation. An instance which might begin as a marginal activity could potentially deteriorate into a genuine emergency compelling congressional support.

Some members of Congress were concerned that the new procedure would have the effect of broadening rather than limiting presidential powers, since in essence it would place a sixty-to-ninety-day stamp of approval on Presidential action,[63] or that for up to ninety days Congress was providing the President with "color of authority" to exercise a war-making power.[64]

The resolution provides for prompt congressional action to avoid unnecessary delays, in the House, in the Senate, and in conference committees to resolve differences between the House and Senate versions. This was included to provide for almost immediate congressional input into any presidential decision to deploy military forces. It was thought that Congress could approve or disapprove every major presidential war powers action almost at the time of its occurrence. Congress was also seeking to avoid a situation in which a President might claim that his acts were in accord with the law and the Constitution, notwithstanding congressional opposition to such acts.

In order to avoid the use of general laws (appropriations, sense of Congress resolutions, and the like) as the basis of presidential troop commitment as Kennedy used them in the Cuban Missile Crisis, the resolution included the statement in Section 8 that no authority was to be inferred from such laws or resolutions unless they constituted a specific statutory authorization; Section 8(a)(2) further added that presidential authority to introduce U.S. forces into hostilities should not be inferred

from any treaty heretofore or hereafter ratified unless such treaty is implemented by legislation specifically authorizing the introduction of United States armed forces into hostilities or into such situations and stating that it is intended to constitute specific statutory authorization within the meaning of this joint resolution.

Under international law this would seem to be an illegal unilateral attempt to change already established treaty commitments. Under both the NATO Treaty and the Rio Treaty, it is provided that an armed attack against any party to the treaty shall be considered as an armed attack against them all and that each member shall come forthwith or immediately to the assistance of the state attacked. This could include the use of armed force.

If international treaties are the supreme law of the land, and if such a treaty states that an attack upon one member is the equivalent of an attack upon the United States, clearly the issue of the President's power to commit forces comes into issue. If the attack were actually on the United States, the President could unquestionably respond with armed force without prior congressional authorization. It can be argued that he has the same right under the treaty, as Commander-in-Chief, to commit U.S. armed forces, and that he certainly has the international law duty to do so, as well as the duty as chief executive faithfully to execute the laws of the land, including treaties.

Irrespective of Section 8(a)(2), which is seemingly unconstitutional, the concluding paragraph of Section 8 affirms that nothing in the resolution is intended to alter the constitutional authority of the Congress or of the President or to alter any provisions of existing treaties.

So it would seem that if a matter is within a President's special competence, such as the interpretation of a collective defense treaty which states that an attack upon one is an attack upon all, Congress has admitted that this Joint Resolution makes no changes in such presidential competence. As has been seen, presidential spokesmen have claimed that major portions of the resolution ill-define the exact perimeters of presidential power to deploy forces without congressional approval.

It can be argued that the most damaging aspect of the War Powers Resolution is its very existence, not the lack of specificity of its provisions. It may remove the threatening imminence of the use of force by an American President as an ace up the presidential sleeve in dealing with other nations. It may thereby allow the leaders of other nations to take it into account without their being bound by the timetables or the procedures set forth in the resolution.

It was left up to the administration of President Ford to preside over the final chapter of United States military involvement in Southeast Asia. Although direct United States participation had ended under Nixon, there was still considerable military support and economic assistance in the pipeline to help the governments in the area in their fight against a communist take-over. But as these funds dried up, no new congressional funds were made available. When the military situation worsened in 1975, Congress refused President Ford's request for additional military funding. Ford thereupon blamed Congress for the impending downfall of South Vietnam and Cambodia, which came about in April, 1975.[65]

As a matter of fact, throughout 1974 and during the first months of 1975 Congress had passed a series of bills restricting the President in his use of various foreign aid and defense appropriations, stating that none of the funds were to be used for the further involvement of American military forces in hostilities in, or over, or from off the shores of Cambodia, Laos, North Vietnam, and South Vietnam.

On April 3, 1975, President Ford began a series of presidential-congressional confrontations on his right to deploy forces without prior consultation. As the Vietnamese lines began to crumble, the President dispatched United States naval vessels and an amphibious task group to the coast of Vietnam to transport refugees from embattled Danang and other seaports to areas farther south which were safer. The next day he sent a report to Congress stating that these military vessels were ordered into the area in order to participate in "an international humanitarian relief effort."[66] This, he said, meant that the operation did not involve "hostilities" under Section 4 (a)(1), and consequently the President was not legally required to consult with Congress under Section 3. Previously, on March 30, President Ford had notified various members of the Senate and House leadership of his intended plans, and he considered that a voluntary gesture of consultation, "although consultation was not technically called for."[67]

On April 10, 1975, in view of the precarious position of remaining embassy personnel in Southeast Asia, the President asked Congress to clarify its statutory funding restrictions to permit him to use United States military forces to evacuate American and foreign nationals from the area. He gave Congress nine days to act and pointed out that the War Powers Resolution, as he read it, gave to the President authority to protect American lives. "To that extent," he said, "I will use the law."[68] Why then ask Congress for further legislative authority? Mainly because he intended to rescue those foreign nationals who had worked closely for many years with the United States and who were therefore prime targets for elimination by the Communists.

Both the House and the Senate agonized trying to find the right language that would give Ford the authority he sought without leading to military reinvolvement in Southeast Asia. A number of congressmen were apprehensive that any legislation, no matter how carefully drafted, would become anachronous and ambiguous because of the rapidly changing situation in the area. The April 19 deadline passed and Congress failed to act, so President Ford went ahead with his evacuations from Cambodia and Vietnam, basing his actions on the presidential executive powers granted by the Constitution, as well as on his authority as Commander-in-Chief. He did not invoke any authority under the War Powers Resolution.[69]

Even though the evacuations were over, Congress continued to debate whether or not to pass the legislation, some members arguing that the President had conducted the evacuations and that Congress should therefore enact legislation to establish the right of Congress to control such actions and to legalize the presidential use of American forces to evacuate our own personnel as well as to evacuate key foreign nationals.

On April 23, both the House and the Senate had passed legislation authorizing this use of funds and of American forces, and the legislation was sent to a joint conference committee. The conference committee moved quickly to resolve House-Senate differences and get the bill to the President, sending the final version of the bill to the House and the Senate on April 24. The Senate approved the conference report the next day, but the House voted it down. And thus this requested authorization ended in an ignominious finale for legislative control over presidential troop commitments.[70]

On April 28, the President directed that congressional leaders should be notified (not consulted) that the "final phase of the evacuation of Saigon would be carried out by means of military forces within the next few hours." In this instance some fighting was involved, and the President met with congressional leaders at the White House to give them a further briefing on the situation in Saigon.[71]

On May 7, the legal adviser of the Department of State testified before a subcommittee of the House International Relations Committee that the Ford administration did not feel that the statutory funding prohibitions applied to presidential action in sending in our armed forces to help in the evacuation.[72] This raises the question of why President Ford had then requested that Congress immediately "clarify" these restrictions. The legal advisor of the Department of State argued that there was substantial legislative history showing that while the 1973 law meant to terminate United States involvement in the war, it was not the intent of Congress in the fund limitations statutes to cut off funding for humanitarian rescue operations; and he added that in any event he thought in such matters as the evacuations there was involved "the inherent constitutional power of the President." "I don't think," he concluded, "that every limitation that Congress might enact on an appropriation or otherwise is necessarily a constitutional one. I think there are some that would be plainly unconstitutional."[73]

Since the Constitution provides that no money shall be drawn from the treasury but in consequence of appropriations made by law, it is difficult to visualize an unconstitutional limitation on appropriations. The supremacy of Congress over the power of the purse was recognized even by the Nixon administration, which asserted possibly the broadest of all presidential constitutional powers to prosecute the war in Vietnam.

If the Ford administration was contending that the President's power to rescue American nationals endangered abroad, as well as non-nationals if that action is operationally linked to the rescue of the Americans, is so inherent that Congress cannot refuse funds for its exercise, this would seem to be a proposition for which there is no constitutional or historical precedent. Furthermore, it would indicate that President Ford felt that his inherent powers would also automatically supersede the War Powers Resolution, which does not have quite the same legal level as an ordinary statute passed through the usual congressional channels.

A possible explanation could be that the Ford administration and its spokesmen were relying on the fact that the President had access to funds other than those involved in the various bills to which the funding restrictions had been attached. This is a doubtful contention at best, for the cost of the evacuations did come from the general defense budget.

Within a few weeks another incident arose in Southeast Asia. Early in the morning of Monday, May 12, 1975, Cambodian communist troops captured the American merchant vessel *Mayaguez* and its crew of 39 in the Gulf of Siam. President Ford responded that afternoon by ordering 100 marines to fly from Okinawa and the Philippines to a United States air base in Thailand, and ordered naval and air force units in the area to join the marines in retaking the ship and its crew members. At 1 A.M. on May 14, United States aircraft sank a number of Cambodian patrol craft, and at 7:20 P.M. of the same day 135 marines landed on Cambodian soil and took possession of the *Mayaguez*. Shortly thereafter American aircraft struck an airfield and an oil storage depot, destroying 17 Cambodian planes and damaging the depot and the runway. In the meantime, Cambodia announced that it was returning the crew, and within a few minutes the destroyer *Wilson* announced that a small boat flying a flag of truce had returned the 39 crew members.[74]

Here again President Ford was faced with the dual limitations passed by Congress in an attempt to curb presidential initiative in the use of force. The first, of course, was the War Powers Resolution, with its hoped-for requirement of prior consultation with Congress, and the second was again Section 30 of the Foreign Assistance Act of 1973, prohibiting further funds expenditure to finance military or para-military operations in Southeast Asia.

In this case, President Ford did not request Congress to clarify any statutory funding prohibitions. And assuming the War Powers Resolution did apply, Ford administration spokesmen said the President had complied with the consultation requirement. Although the *Mayaguez* incident was a rapidly unfolding emergency situation, a number of separate sets of communications took place between the executive branch and the congressional leadership. These included a dozen telephone calls by members of the White House staff to leaders of the House and Senate early in the evening of May 13 informing them of the situation, a State Department briefing of members of three congressional committees on the situation, and a meeting on the 14th of the President with the congressional leadership, at which time Ford described the specific orders that he had given for recapture of the ship and crew.[75] None of the congressional members who were telephoned or briefed, or who met with the President, apparently made any sort of protest regarding his actions. About half verbally approved, and the rest merely acknowledged the information received.[76] On the other hand, President Ford did not openly invite a discussion on the pros and cons of his decision to intervene. He was "extremely apprehensive that there be no breach of security in advance of the time that they [the troops] actually were landed, so there were strong arguments for not revealing that information—even to a select group of members—very much in advance of the time it was to occur."[77]

Nevertheless, a number of congressmen were later critical about the lack of consultation. The *New York Times* reported that Senate Majority Leader Mike Mansfield, the ranking member of the Senate Foreign Relations Committee, reported on May 15, "I was not consulted. I was notified after the fact about what the administration had already decided to do. I did not give my approval or disapproval because the decision had already been made."[78] To which an administration spokesman replied: "It is easy to envision some circumstances where compliance might be difficult, even when the executive is making a good faith effort to comply. The difference is likely to be a matter of interpretation."[79] This was echoed by some members of Congress who recognized that there was a good deal of honest difference of opinion on what precisely the consultation provision called for and what Congress intended when the act was adopted. Senator Jacob Javits, who helped draft the bill, told a June 4 hearing of the House International Relations Subcommittee on International Security and Scientific Affairs that he believed the rescue of the vessel and crew fell within the emergency powers of the President, thus fitting into one of the categories of the law in which the President could commit troops abroad.[80] He added that he thought the law had stood up well in its initial tests, although the consultation provision was the pressure point most vulnerable to circumvention and manipulation.

On May 15, President Ford submitted his report on the *Mayaguez* to Congress, stating that in doing so he was taking note of Section 4 (a)(1) of the War Powers Resolution which requires the President to submit such a report within forty-eight hours. He neglected to invoke Section 4 (a)(3) which also requires such a report when there is a substantial enlargement of combat-ready forces at a foreign base, in this case the additional marines sent to Thailand. It may be that he did not consider one hundred marines a sufficiently "substantial" number to require such reporting. In his report Ford outlined the sequence of events that led to the use of United States armed forces, highlighting the fact that the Cambodian seizure of the ship was "in clear violation of international law."[81] But he did not base his actions on such presidential powers as may still remain under international law, that is, the right of self-defense in face of a direct armed attack. He declared that his action was taken under his constitutional authority to protect American lives and as Commander-in-Chief.[82]

His report stressed that the actions taken were done in good faith, and he did not acknowledge that either the funding restrictions or the War Powers Resolution applied; rather, he maintained that he was acting under his own constitutionally granted powers. The implication was clear that Ford wanted to avoid provoking a theoretical confrontation with Congress over the War Powers Resolution, but at the same time wished to keep presidential options open for future use of troops.

Although congressional reaction to both the evacuations and the *Mayaguez* incident was generally favorable, there still remains the unanswered question of whether or not President Ford in any way usurped the congressional power over the purse by ignoring the funding restrictions. As Congress permitted such usurpation in these cases, they can be cited by future Presidents as precedents for military operations for which Congress has denied funds.

The *Mayaguez* incident demonstrated that neither the funding limitation nor the War Powers Resolution had diminished the ability of the President to act decisively in committing troops abroad. Military actions in modern times can take far less than even forty-eight hours, to say nothing of the 60-90 day limitation. So when such quick action is needed it would seem the War Powers Resolution presents no real or substantial limitation on presidential powers, whether they flow from the power as Commander-in-Chief or from any other power or group of powers under constitutional or international law.

Following the *Mayaguez* incident, there were attempts to amend the War Powers Resolution by clarifying the consultation provision. Senator Thomas Eagleton also introduced legislation explicitly recognizing the President's right to protect American lives (not property), and stipulating various conditions limiting this power: that the citizens to be rescued would have to be involuntarily held with the express or tacit consent of the foreign government; that there would have to be direct and imminent threat to their lives; and that the evacuations would have to take place as expeditiously as possible with a minimum use of force. But Eagleton's proposal, along with attempts to clarify the meaning of consultation, were not acted upon by Congress.[83]

Early in his administration, President Carter was questioned on his views of the War Powers Resolution. He acknowledged that it was an attempted reduction of presidential powers, but declared that he would have "no hesitancy about communicating with Congress, consulting with them . . . before we start any combat operation."[84] But when the crunch came, he followed in the footsteps of former President Gerald Ford.

On November 4, 1979, a group of militant Iranians overran the American Embassy in Tehran and held in captivity all the Americans found in the buildings of the Embassy compound. In spite of this clear violation of international law as to the sanctity of diplomatic missions, denounced by most nations of the world and by a unanimous decision of the International Court of Justice,[85] the Iranian government refused to intervene to release the American hostages. After five months of fruitless negotiation, President Jimmy Carter became impatient with the inability or unwillingness of the Iranian government to return the Americans and determined to take military action.

On April 24, 1980, elements of the United States Armed Forces were alerted to proceed with the rescue of the American hostages. Six United States C-130 transport aircraft and eight RH-53 helicopters entered Iran airspace. Their crews were not equipped for combat. But some of the C-130 aircraft carried a force of approximately ninety members of the rescue team, equipped for combat, plus various support personnel. During the flight to a rendezvous at a remote desert site approximately two hundred miles from Tehran, three of the helicopters developed operating difficulties. At the rendezvous site, one of the helicopters crashed into a C-130, resulting in the death of eight men and serious injury to three. Because six helicopters would have been needed to complete the mission, Carter, at the advice of his military advisers, decided to cancel the operation and ordered the United States armed forces involved to return from Iran.[86]

The remote desert area was selected to conceal the mission from immediate discovery. At no time during the temporary presence of the United States armed forces in Iran did they encounter Iranian forces. They did encounter two trucks and a busload of forty-four Iranian civilians on a road near the site. The bus was stopped and the civilians were detained until the United States armed forces departed. The first truck was stopped by shooting out its headlights, but the driver dashed to the second truck and this truck escaped.[87]

On April 26 Carter reported to the Speaker of the House and the President Pro Tempore of the Senate on the unsuccessful operation. While he declared that it was his desire that Congress be informed on this matter "consistent with the reporting provisions of the War Powers Resolution of 1973," nonetheless he concluded that the operation was "ordered and conducted pursuant to the President's power under the Constitution as chief executive and as Commander-in-Chief," expressly recognized in Section 8(d)(1) of the War Powers Resolution, i.e., the section which states that nothing in the joint resolution is intended to alter the constitutional authority of the Congress or of the President.[88]

President Carter also pointed out that the United States was acting wholly within its right, in accordance with Article 51 of the United Nations Charter, to protect and rescue its citizens where the government of the territory in which they were located was unwilling or unable to protect them.[89]

President Carter, like President Ford before him, took care to notify Congress that he was acting in the exercise of his inherent presidential powers, pursuant to the constitutional power both as the nation's chief executive in the conduct of foreign affairs and under his authority as Commander-in-Chief. He felt no legal obligation, therefore, to consult with Congress before taking action; and like President Ford's report on actions in Southeast Asia, Carter's report reads more like an act of presidential courtesy to Congress than the fulfilling of a legal restriction placed upon presidential powers by law of Congress.

In September, 1982, the government of Lebanon, in face of continued civil strife and armed conflict caused by the presence on Lebanese soil of the amed forces of the Palestine Liberation Army, the armed forces of Israel, and the armed forces of Syria, requested the governments of France, Italy, and the United States to contribute forces to serve as a temporary multinational force in that nation. It was hoped that the presence of such a multinational force would help the Lebanese government regain full sovereignty and authority throughout that country. In response to this request, President Reagan, without consulting Congress, agreed to send 1,200 marines into Lebanon. Nine days later, in a letter to the Speaker of the House and the President Pro Tempore of the Senate, the President stated that it was his desire that Congress be fully informed on this matter, and therefore, consistent with the War Powers Resolution, he was providing a report on the deployment and mission of the marines. President Reagan pointed out in the letter that in his agreement with the Lebanese government any combat responsibilities for the marines were expressly ruled out, but he emphasized that they would be equipped for, and permitted if necessary, actions in the right of self-defense. Again, like Presidents Ford and Carter, Reagan stressed that his deployment of these armed forces was "being undertaken pursuant to the President's constitutional authority with respect to the conduct of foreign relations and as Commander-in-Chief of the United States armed forces."[90]

Indeed, in all the instances where the War Powers Resolution has come into play since its passage, there has been no cutting back on the assertion of the power of the President to use force for the redress of alleged wrongs against American citizens and property, abroad or on the high seas, to evacuate non-Americans under humanitarian intervention, or to intervene to end civil or international strife abroad. In the future, other types of crises may arise which were not anticipated by the War Powers Resolution, and probably no President would refuse effectively to defend what he thought was the country's best interest in favor of a liberal compliance with the resolution as seen through the eyes of many congressmen.

All in all, the power of the President to commit forces abroad remains a dark continent of American jurisprudence.

NOTES

INTRODUCTION

1. The number of such military ventures is seemingly a subject of some dispute. One commentator writing in 1945 states that between the years 1789 and 1945 the President, acting upon his own authority, used force abroad at least 80 times. J. Rogers, World Policing and the Constitution 92-123 (1945). In 1951 a Senate committee report said that the President had ordered the use of troops abroad without congressional authorization at least 125 times. Study prepared for the use of the joint committee made up of the Committee on Foreign Relations and the Committee on Armed Services of the Senate, 82nd Cong., 1st Sess., Powers of the President to Send the Armed Forces outside the United States, Feb. 28, 1951. Quincy Wright speaks of something more than 170 such incidents. See Wright, "The Power of the Executive to Use Military Forces Abroad," 10 Va. J. Int'l Law 42 at 48 (1969).

2. As quoted in A. Schlesinger, Jr., The Imperial Presidency 138 (1973).

3. W. Taft, Our Chief Magistrate and His Powers 128-29 (1916).

4. As quoted in Schlesinger, *supra* note 2, at 138.

5. Cong. Rec., April 26, 1971, S5639.

6. 7 The Writings of Thomas Jefferson 461 (Literary ed. 1903).

7. 1 A. Lincoln, Collected Works, 451-52 (Basler, ed. 1953).

8. See E. Corwin, The President: Office and Powers 229 (4th rev. ed. 1957).

9. R. Taft, A Foreign Policy for Americans 31 (1951).

10. National Commitments, Sen. Res. No. 797, 90th Cong., 1st Sess. (1967), as quoted in G. Gunther, Constitutional Law Cases and Materials 417 (10th ed. 1980).

11. Fulbright, "American Foreign Policy in the 20th Century under an 18th Century Constitution," 47 Cornell L.Q. 1 (1961).

147

12. A. Schlesinger, Jr., "Congress and the Making of Foreign Policy," in R. Tugwell and T. Cronin (editors) The Presidency Re-Appraised 110 (1974).

13. 299 U.S. 304, 320 (1936).

14. For discussions of these various reasons pro and con presidential power, see statements made in National Commitments Hearing, *supra* note 10; Velvel, "The War in Viet Nam: Unconstitutional, Justiciable, and Jurisdictionally Attackable," 16 Kan. L. Rev. 449 (1968); Hoxie, "The Office of Commander in Chief: An Historical and Projective View," 6 Presidential Studies Quarterly 10 (1976); A. Schlesinger, Jr., The Imperial Presidency, chap. 9 (1973); Reveley, "Presidential War-Making: Constitutional Prerogative or Usurpation?" 55 Va. L. Rev. 1243, at 543 *et seq.* (1969).

CHAPTER ONE

1. The Articles of Confederation may be found in H. Taylor, The Origin & Growth of the American Constitution 517.

2. Art. VI.

3. *Id.*

4. Art. IX.

5. Art. X.

6. See the influence of the rebellion in the words of James Madison. 3 M. Farrand (ed.) The Records of the Federal Convention of 1787, 539 (rev. ed. 1966); see also A. Sofaer, War, Foreign Affairs and Constitutional Powers—The Origin 18 (1974).

7. On the ineffectuality of the Articles of Confederation and the factors prompting the founding fathers to a new Constitution see C. Beard, American Government and Politics chap. 3 (1914).

8. 4 Farrand, *supra* note 6, at 59.

9. 2 Farrand, *id.* at 617.

10. *Id.* at 329, 332, 382, 386, 388, 509.

11. Russell F. Weigley, History of the United States Army 81 (1967).

12. 2 Farrand, *supra* note 6, at 341.

13. U.S. Const., Art. XII. See also 1 The Federalist 135 (Scott ed. 1894).

14. 3 Farrand, *supra* note 7, at 622.

15. 2 Farrand, *supra* note 7, at 318.

16. Jane Butzner, Constitutional Chaff 63 (1941); Arthur T. Prescott, Drafting the Federal Constitution 515 (1968).

17. U.S. Const. Art. I, Sec. 3.

18. Farrand, *supra* note 7, at 318.

19. See Corwin's quotations from Blackstone, Locke, and Montesquieu on these powers of the king. E. Corwin, The President: Office and Powers, 1787-1957, 416-17 (1957).

20. Farrand, *supra* note 6, at 318-19.

21. U.S. Const. Art. II, Sec. 2.

22. *Id.*

23. 2 Farrand, *supra* note 6, at 540.

24. *Id.* at 183.

25. 3 Farrand, *supra* note 6, at 250.

26. 2 Farrand, *supra* note 6, at 548.

27. *Id.* at 394.

28. *Id.*

29. *Id.* at 548.

30. *Id.*

31. U.S. Const., Art. II, Sec. 2.

32. *Id.* Art. I, Sec. 8.

33. *Id.* Art. II, Sec. 2.

34. *Id.* Art. I, Sec. 8.

35. *Id.*, Art. II, Sec. 2.

36. Art. II, Sec. 2, Par. 2.

37. Art. I, Sec. 8, Par. 11 & Art. I, Sec. 7, Par. 2.

38. Art. II, Sec. 2, Par. 1.

39. J. Terry Emerson, "Constitutional Authority of the President to Use Armed Force in Defense of American Lives, Liberty and Property," 121 Cong. Rec. S7526 (Daily ed. May 6, 1975); Milton Offritt, "The Protection of Citizens Abroad by the Armed Forces of the United States," Johns Hopkins Univ. Studies in Hist. & Pol. Sci. Series XLIV, No. 4, 32 (1928); Francis D. Wormuth, "The Nixon Theory of the War Power: A Critique," 60 Calif. Law Rev. 648 (1972); Raoul Beyer, "War-Making by the President," 121 Univ. of Penn. Law Rev. 69 (1972); Note, "Congress, the President and the Power to Commit Forces to Combat," 81 Harvard Law Rev. 1771 (1981); A. Bickel, "Congress, The President, and the Power to Declare War," 48 Chicago Kent Law Rev. 137 (1971); A. Bickel, "The Constitution and War," July 1972 Commentary 51; Leonard C. Meeker, "The Legality of the United States Participation—the Defense of Vietnam," 54 Dept. State Bull. 474 (March 3, 1966); Jacob Javits, Who Makes War? (1973); Thomas Eagleton, War and Presidential Power (1974).

40. As stated by Mr. Justice Frankfurter in his concurring opinion in Youngstown Sheet and Tube Co. v. Sawyer, 343 U.S. 579 (1952):

It is an inadmissibly narrow conception of American constitutional law to confine it to the words of the Constitution and to disregard the gloss which life has written upon them. In short, a systematic, unbroken, executive practice, long pursued to the knowledge of the Congress and never before questioned, engaged in by the Presidents who have also sworn to uphold the Constitution, making as it were such exercise of power part of the structure of our government, may be treated as a gloss on "executive Power" vested in the President by §1 of Art. II.

CHAPTER TWO

1. An excellent study concerning constitutional problems of war and peace and the use of force from the time of the coming into effect of the Constitution until 1829 is that of A. Sofaer, War, Foreign Affairs and Constitutional Powers: The Origins (1976). Francis D. Wormuth has also given us an excellent study of the historical uses of force by the government of the United States. See Wormuth, "The Vietnam War: The President versus the Constitution," 2 The Vietnam War and International Law 711 (Falk ed. 1969); A Schlesinger, Jr., in his work, The Imperial Presidency (1973) also gives an interesting account of presidential uses of force throughout United States history.

2. The incident is related in Sofaer, *id.* at 103 *et seq.*

3. 7 Hamilton Works, 76-83, 15 The Papers of Alexander Hamilton 33-40 (H. Syrett ed. 1961).

4. Madison, Writings 153, 158-59, 174-82 (G. Hunt ed. 1906).

5. For discussion of this undeclared war see Sofaer, *supra* note 1, at 139 *et seq.* See also Wormuth, *supra* note 1, at 718 *et seq.* On the Supreme Court decisions and discussion thereof see *infra* pp. 42-44.

6. On this episode see Sofaer, *id.* at 208 *et seq.*; and see *infra* pp. 52-53.

7. No. 1 of "Lucius Crassus," Dec. 17, 1801, Alexander Hamilton and the Founding of the Nation 526 (R. Morris ed. 1957).

8. He had said that history demonstrated that the executive power "is the branch of power most interested in war, and most prone to it." Madison to Jefferson, April 2, 1798, 6 Madison, Writings, 312-13 (G. Hunt ed. 1906).

9. Although the nation was divided as to the war issue, a group of "War Hawks" congressmen from the western states, in control of the House, were able to

bring the nation to war to advance western interests. The epoch is well described in J. Javits, Who Makes War? chap. 6 (1974).

10. Sofaer, *supra* note 1, at 270.

11. *Id.* at 351-53. For detailed account of this period and presidential use of force see *id.* chap. 5.

12. See J. Rogers, World Policing and the Constitution (1945); and see U.S. Department of State, Right to Protect Citizens in Foreign Countries by Landing Forces, Memorandum of the Solicitor of the Department of State 23-24, 40, 44, 48 (3d rev. ed. 1934).

13. For legal discussion see *infra* chap. 6.

14. Hoxie, "The Office of Commander-in-Chief: An Historical and Prospective View," 6 Presidential Studies Quarterly 10 at 14 (1976).

15. Adams to Gallatin, Dec. 26, 1847, as set forth in S. Bemis, John Quincy Adams and the Union 499 (1956).

16. Congressional Globe, 30th Cong. 1st Sess. (Jan. 3, 1848), p. 95.

17. See 1 A. Lincoln, Collected Works 451-52 (Basler ed. 1953).

18. As summarized in E. Corwin, The President: Office and Powers 1787-1957, 229 *et seq.* (1957).

19. This is a view taken by Schlesinger, *supra* note 1, at 82. Javits, *supra* note 9, at 150-51 casts some doubt on this proposition, intimating that the war might well have been instigated by President McKinley, who gave an appearance of reluctance to war.

CHAPTER THREE

1. For discussion of the Boxer intervention see F. Grob, The Relativity of War and Peace, 64-79 (1949); J. Rogers, World Policy and the Constitution, 59-62 (1945); S. Bemis, A Diplomatic History of the United States 486-88 (5th ed. 1965).

2. However, a federal court did find that war existed even though there had been no formal declaration by the United States Congress. Hamilton v. McClaughey, Warden 136 Fed. 445 (C.C.D. Kan. 1905).

3. For discussion of this intervention and its background see C. Martin, The Policy of the United States as Regards Intervention, 162 *et seq.* (1921). Bemis, *supra* note 1, at 512; G. Stuart, Latin America and the United States chap. 5 (4th ed. 1943).

4. 3 Moore's, A Digest of International Law 46 (1906).

5. *Id.* at 71.

6. Quoted in H. Pringle, Theodore Roosevelt 318 (1913); D. Graber, Crisis Diplomacy 139 (1959).

7. See A. V. W. Thomas and A. J. Thomas, Jr., Non-Intervention: The Law and Its Import in the Americas, chap. 2 (1956).

8. Joint Resolution of Congress, April 20, 1898, as contained in 6 Moore's Digest of International Law 225 *et seq.* (1906).

9. 1 Malloy's Treaties 364 (1910).

10. An act to make appropriation for the Army for the fiscal year ending June 30, 1902, 31 Stat. 897 (1901).

11. See Thomas and Thomas, *supra* note 7, 24-28.

12. *Id.* at 28.

13. Foreign Relations of the United States 1913, 7.

14. *Id.*, 1914, 447. For a background and summary of this incident, see Address of President Wilson before the United States Congress on the Situation of Our Dealing with General Victoriano Huerta, April 20, 1914, in J. Richardson, 16 Messages and Papers of the President 7934 (no date).

15. *Id.* at 7936.

16. These incidents and the action taken are recorded by Robert Lansing. See Secretary of State, in A Message to the Government of Mexico, June 20, 1916, Foreign Relations of the United States 1916, 581.

17. See President Roosevelt's Message to the Senate, Feb. 15, 1905, as set forth in 6 Moore's Digest of International Law 518 *et seq.* (1906).

18. This treaty is set forth in 1 Am. J. Int'l Law Supp. 231 (1907).

19. See Thomas and Thomas, *supra* note 7, at 34-36. For a complete account of the entire interventionary period see S. Welles, Naboth's Vineyard, The Dominican Republic 1844-1924 (1928).

20. See Thomas and Thomas, *supra* note 7, at 36-39. See also A. Buell, The American Occupation of Haiti, Foreign Policy Association, Information Service, 5, nos. 19-20, 1929.

21. See 2 Moore's Digest 113-14, 181 (1906); Rogers, *supra* note 7, at 38-39.

22. Foreign Relations of the United States 1910, 455 and xvii; see also Right to Protect Citizens in Foreign Countries by Landing Forces, *supra* note 7 at 75-77.

23. D. Perkins, Hands Off, A History of the Monroe Doctrine 941, 25; Foreign Relations of the United States 1912, 1032.

24. A Message from President Calvin Coolidge to the U.S. Congress, Jan. 10, 1927, Foreign Relations of the United States, 1927, III 288.

25. He claimed authority to resort to armed neutrality under an old statute. See Bemis, *supra* note 1, at 612, and J. Javits, Who Makes War? 203 (1973).

26. On these ventures see Bemis, *id.* at 641 *et seq.*; D. Graber, Crisis Diplomacy 185 *et seq.* (1959); A. Schlesinger, Jr., The Imperial Presidency 93 (1973); E. Corwin, The President: Office and Powers 178, 195, 464 n. 90 (1957).

27. These acts and others of President Roosevelt are set forth in Corwin, *id.* at 202-3.

28. *Id.* at 204.

CHAPTER FOUR

1. Resolution of the Security Council, 25 June 1950, S/1501, SCOR, V, Resolutions and Decisions, 1950 (S/INF/5/Rev. 1), pp. 4-5; Resolution of the Security Council, 27 June 1950, S/1511, SCOR, V, Resolutions and Decisions, 1950 (S/INF/4/Rev. 1), p. 5.

2. Resolution of the Security Council, 7 July 1950, S/1588, SCOR, V, Resolutions and Decisions, 1950 (S/INF/5/Rev. 1) p. 5.

3. Resolution 498 (V) of the General Assembly, 1 February 1951, GAOR, V, Supp. 20A (A/1775/Cdd 1), p. 1.

4. See on these aspects: U.S. Dept. of State, Authority of the President to Repel the Attack in Korea, 23 Dept. State Bull. 173 (1950); Hoyt, "The United States Reaction to the Korean Attack, a Study of the Principles of the United Nations Charter as a Factor in American Policy-Making," 55 Am. J. Int'l L. 45 (1961); A. Schlesinger, Jr., The Imperial Presidency, 130 *et seq.* (1973); J. Moore, The National Executive and the Use of Force Abroad, Law and the Indo-China War, 538 at 544-45 (1972); L. Goodrich, Korea, A Study of U.S. Foreign Policy chap. 5 (1956).

5. U.S. Dept. of State, Authority of the President, *id.* at 173. Acheson, "Act of Aggression in Korea," 23 Dept. State Bull. 48 (1940).

6. "Authority of the President to Repel the Attack in Korea," 23 Dept. State Bull. 173-74 (1950).

7. *Id.*

8. "Power of the President to Send Armed Forces Outside the United States," Senate Comm. on For. Rel. & Armed Services, 82nd Cong., 1st Sess. pp. 2-3, 20-22, Feb. 28, 1957. See Lofgren, "Mr. Truman's War: A Debate and Its Aftermath," 31 Rev. of Pol. 231 (1969).

9. As quoted in Schlesinger, *supra* note 4, at 138.

10. For discussion see *infra* pp. 82-83.

11. See Schlesinger, *supra* note 4, at 135-40.

12. N.Y. Times, Oct. 30, 1956.

13. 101 Cong. Rec. 601, Jan. 24, 1955.

14. As set forth in J. Javits, Who Makes War? 255 (1973).

15. As noted in Schlesinger, *supra* note 4, at 161.

16. As quoted in L. Sohn, Cases on United Nations Law 680 (2d ed. rev. 1967).

17. 102 Cong. Rec. 13, 903-4 "Statement of the President," July 15, 1958.

18. N.Y. Times, May 9, 1960.

19. N.Y. Times, April 20, 1961.

20. T. Sorenson, Kennedy 702 (1965).

21. Pres. Proc. No. 3540, 27 Fed. Reg. 10, 401 (Oct. 23, 1922).

22. Pub. Q. No. 87-733, 76 Stat. 697, Oct. 3, 1962.

23. "The Address of the President, The Soviet Threats to the Americas," 47 Dept. State Bull. 715 (1962).

24. P.A.U., The Council of the Organization of American States Acting Provisionally as Organ of Consultation, Council Series O.E.A./Ser. G./V, C-D-1024 (English) Rev. 23 Oct. 1962.

25. Statement by President Kennedy, News Conference, Sept. 13, 1962, N.Y. Times, Sept. 14, 1962.

26. *Id.*

27. Sorenson, *supra* note 20, at Kennedy, 702.

28. War Powers Legislation, Hearings before Senate Committee, p. 91, 92nd Cong., 1st Sess. (1971).

29. See statements of the U.S. Government, 51 Dept. State Bull. 838-46 (1964).

30. As set forth in the First Report of the Special Committee, 4 International Legal Materials 557 at 565 (May 1965).

31. This request for assistance has been a subject of controversy. See Comments on the Dominican Republic by Senator Fulbright, Cong. Rec., 89th Cong., 1st Sess., Vol. III, No. 198-Pt. 2, Oct. 22, 1965.

32. Statement by President Johnson, April 28, 52 Dept. State Bull. 738 (1965).

33. Address by the Honorable Thomas C. Mann, Dept. State Press Release 241, Oct. 12, 1965, and see A. V. W. Thomas and A. J. Thomas, Jr., The Dominican Republic Crisis 1965, 7 (Hammarskjold Forum 1967).

34. 1 The O.A.S. Chronicle 23-24 (Aug. 1965). See also Thomas and Thomas *id.* at 36 *et seq.*

35. On the U.S. involvement, see Bundy, "The Path to Viet-Nam: A Lesson in Involvement," 1 Falk, The Viet-Nam War and International Law 13 (1969). Javits, *supra* note 14, at 257; A. Schlesinger, Jr., The Bitter Heritage: Vietnam and American Democracy 1941-1966 (1967); J. McCarthy, Illusion of Power in Viet-Nam (1967).

36. N. Sheehan and Others, The Pentagon Papers 189-92 (1971). See also Katzenbach, "Congress and Foreign Policy," 3 Falk, The Vietnam War and International Law 596 at 601 (1972). On the Johnson policy see Schlesinger, *supra* note 4, chap. 7.

37. See Statement of Undersecretary Katzenbach, U.S. Commitments to Foreign Powers, Hearings before the Committee on Foreign Relations of the United States Senate, 90th Cong., 1st Sess. 9, 80-81, 161, 174 (1967).

38. Meeker, "The Legality of U.S. Participation in the Defense of Vietnam," 54 Dept. State Bull. 474 (1966).

39. Joint Resolution of Aug. 10, 1964. Pub. Law No. 88-408, 78 Stat. 384 (1964).

40. Meeker, *supra* note 38, at 489. See also Bickel, "Congress, the President and the Power to Declare War," 48 Chicago-Kent L. Rev. 137 at 139 (1971).

41. Hoxie, "The Office of Commander-in-Chief, An Historical and Prospective View," 6 Presidential Studies Quarterly 10 at 25 (No. 4, Fall 1976).

42. Schlesinger, *supra* note 4, at 181.

43. 209 U.N.T.S. 28 (1955).

44. U.S. Commitments to Foreign Powers, Hearings Before the Committee on Foreign Relations of the United States, 90th Cong., 1st Sess. 82 (1967).

45. Meeker, *supra* note 38.

46. See Memorandum of Law by Lawyers Committee on American Policy Towards Vietnam, September 1965, U.S. Senate Committee on Foreign Relations, Hearings on S. 2793; Supplemental Foreign Assistance Fiscal Year 1966—Vietnam, 89th Cong., 2d Sess. 687 (1966); Lawyers Committee Reply to the State Department, Oct. 1966, 112 Cong. Rec. A 5801 (1966-67).

47. Message of May 4, ¶ 65, Senate Comm. on For. Relations, Background Information Relating to Southeast Asia & Vietnam, 89th Cong., 1st Sess. 219. Comm. Print Rev. ed. 1965.

48. Moore & Underwood, The Lawfulness of U.S. Assistance to the Republic of Vietnam, 112 Cong. Rec. 15519 at 63-77 (1968).

49. The Text of the Paris Agreement is found in 68 Dept. State Bull. 169 (1973).

50. President Nixon's Address to the Nation on "Military Actions in Cambodia," April 30, 1970, as contained in 3 Falk, The Vietnam War and International Law 865 at 869 (1972).

51. Hoxie, *supra* note 41, at 24.

52. 84 Stat. 2053 (1971).

53. Spokesmen of the Nixon Administration set forth the idea that the administration did not depend on the resolution for constitutional authority. See Cong. Rec. April 2, 1973, S6287.

54. See Hoxie, *supra* note 41, at 25. 87 Stat. 99 (1973).

55. 87 Stat. 555, Public Law 93-148, 93d Cong. (1973). As to the presidential veto, see Message of Oct. 23, 1973, H. Doc. No. 93-171, 119 Cong. Rec. H0488. See also Ehrlich, "The Legal Process in Foreign Affairs: Military Intervention—A Testing Case," 27 Stanford L. Rev. 657, 648 (1978). See *infra* chap. 6 for discussion.

56. See G. Gunther, Constitutional Law Cases and Materials 416 (10th ed. 1975); Eagleton, "Congress's Inaction on War," N.Y. Times, May 6, 1975.

57. Gunther, *id.*

58. President Ford did comply with the requirement of the resolution that a written report be submitted to Congress within forty-eight hours. Schlesinger, however, states that the President commenced a small war without congressional authority. Schlesinger, "Is the Presidency Too Powerful?" Readers Digest Dec. 1975, p. 88.

CHAPTER FIVE

1. For summaries of certain of the presidential statements in this regard see Berger, "War-Making by the President," 121 Pa. L. Rev. 29 at 61-66 (1971); Wormuth, "The Vietnam War versus the Constitution," as set forth in Falk, 2 The Vietnam War and International Law 711 at 737-41 (1969); Putney, "Executive Assumption of the War Making Power," 7 Nat'l L. Rev. 1, 6-30 (1927).

2. On this episode see *supra* pp. 10-11 and *infra* pp. 82-83.

3. Messages and Papers of the Presidents 1789-1897 at 376-77 (J. Richardson ed. 1907).

4. As quoted in Putney, *supra* note 1, at 9.

5. See *supra* p. 10.

6. As quoted in Wormuth, *supra* note 1, at 738.

7. See Putney, *supra* note 1, at 12.

8. *Id.* at 31.

9. On this incident see Wormuth, *supra* note 1, at 939.

10. As quoted in Putney, *supra* note 1, at 15.

11. See *supra* p. 11.

12. As discussed in Putney, *supra* note 1, at 18.

13. *Id.* at 23-24.

14. *Id.* at 25.

15. See Berger, *supra* note 1, at 641.

16. See *supra* pp. 14-16.

17. It has been said that two-thirds of the members of Congress would have opposed World War II the day before Pearl Harbor. See Berger, *supra* note 1, at 641.

18. E. Corwin, The President, Office and Powers, 201 (4th rev. ed. 1957).

CHAPTER SIX

1. Art. I, sec. 8.

2. See discussions in chaps. 2, 3, and 4 *supra.*

3. C. Fenwick, International Law (3d ed. 1952), traces briefly at page 552 the historical practices of nations which prevailed concerning the declaration of war. He states that in more modern times the practice of declaration or giving formal notice has tended to fall into disuse.

4. Hearing on S. Res. 151, National Commitments, 90th Cong., 1st Sess., 161-62 (1967).

5. See *supra* n. 1, Introduction.

6. War of 1812, Mexican War, Spanish American War, World War I, World War II. And see J. Rogers, World Policy and the Constitution 45 (1954).

7. Works of Alexander Hamilton 249-50 (Henry Cabot Lodge ed., 2d 1903).

8. On the discussion at the Constitutional Convention see 2 M. Farrand, The Records of the Federal Convention of 1787, 318 *et seq.* (rev. ed. 1973).

9. J. Story, Commentaries on the Constitution 410-11 (1833). Lofgren in an article entitled "War-Making under the Constitution: The Original Understanding," 81 Yale L.J. 672 (1972) points out at 687-97 that the power granted to the Congress to grant letters of marque and reprisal reinforced the founding fathers' probable intentions that the Congress should control all war whether declared or undeclared, legal or material or imperfect. At the time of the drafting of the Constitution the term was understood to signify a commission granted by a government to a private person to fit out an armed vessel to cruise at sea and capture ships and cargoes belonging to citizens of another state. Grob, *infra* note 19, at 239. Such letters could be issued in time of war or peace, and because they also involved use of force to be authorized by Congress, it was believed to be suggested that all or almost all uses of force should be so authorized. Lofgren tells us at 700 that contemporaries of the framers were probably convinced that "Congress would have nearly complete authority over the commencement of war . . ." because of its power to declare war and to grant letters of marque and reprisal.

10. See 10 M. Whiteman, A Digest of International Law 1 (1968); J. Stone, Legal Controls of International Conflict 304-6 (1954); Q. Wright, The Control of American Foreign Relations 284 (1922); H. Grotius viewed war as a status or condition. H. Grotius, De Jure Belli ae Pacis, Bk. I, chap. I sec. 2 (1646 ed.). The Classics of International Law 33 (ed. Scott 1925).

11. E. de Vattel, The Law of Nations or the Principles of National Law, Bk. III, chap. 1 (1758). The Classics of International Law 235 (ed. Scott 1925).

12. 4 U.S. (4 Dall.) 37 (1800).

13. *Id.* at 40.

14. 2 Oppenheim, International Law, Disputes, War and Neutrality 202 (7th ed. Lauterpacht 1952).

15. Wright, "When Does War Exist?" 26 Am. J. Int. L. 362 (1930).

16. Stone, *supra* note 10, at 304.

17. On the *animus belligerendi* see Stone, *id.* at 304-6; Brierly, "International Law and Resort to Armed Force," 4 Cambridge L. Rev. 308 at 311-14 (1932); McNair, "The Legal Meaning of War, and the Relation of War to Reprisals," 11 The Grotius Soc. at 29-35 (1926); H. Kelsen, Principles of International Law 22-25 (2d ed. Tucker (1966)).

18. Wright, *supra* note 15, at 365.

19. For discussion of the concepts see L. Kotzsch, The Concepts of War in Contemporary History and International Law chap. 3 (1956); F. Grob, The Relativity of War and Peace chaps. 6 and 7 (1949).

20. Brierly, *supra* note 17, at 313.

21. Kotzsch, *supra* note 19, at 53-65.

22. *Id.*

23. Kotzsch points out that most all of the publicists from Grotius up to World War I viewed war as a status. *Id.* at 39.

24. 4 U.S. (4 Dall.) 39-41.

25. *Id.* at 42.

26. 6 U.S. (2 Cranch) 170 (1804).

27. *Id.* at 174.

28. 67 U.S. (2 Black) 635 (1863).

29. *Id.* at 689-90.

30. For a description of pacific blockade as force short of war see 2 Oppenheim, *supra* note 14, at 144 *et seq.*; J. Starke, An Introduction to International Law 290 *et seq.* (5th ed. 1963).

31. On this period of United States history see A. Sofaer, War, Foreign Affairs and Constitutional Power: The Origins, chap. 3 (1975); *see also* Grob, *supra* note 19, at 33 *et seq.*

32. 23 Stat. 283 (1885).

33. Grob, *supra* note 19, at 56.

34. 21 Ct. Cl. 340 (1886).

35. *Id.* at 374-75.

36. See, e.g., Cushing, Administrator v. the United States, 22 Ct. Cl. 1 (1886); Hooper, Administrator v. U.S. 22 Ct. Cl. 408 (1887); The Ship Concord v. the United States, 22 Ct. Cl. 442 (1900).

37. Velvel, "The War in Vietnam: Unconstitutional, Justiciable, and Jurisdictionally Attackable," 16 Kan. L. Rev. 449 (1968). Velvel would permit the President to use force to repel sudden attack, but within a limited time thereafter he should obtain a limited or general declaration of war from Congress. See also Wormuth, "The Vietnam War: The President Versus the Constitution," 1 Study of Democratic Institutions 2 (1968) as set forth in 2 Falk, The Vietnam War and International Law 711 (1969); Lofgren, "War-Making under the Constitution: The Original Understanding," 81 Yale L.J. 672 (1972). This author, in an excellent article, points out that the founding fathers probably intended that Congress should commence all uses of force except possibly defensive uses. Berger concludes that the war-making power rests in the Congress. The President can repel sudden attacks on the United States. Berger, "War-Making Power by the President," 212 U. Penn. L. Rev. 29 (1971).

38. Certain publicists taking such a position are Wright, "The Power of the Executive to Use Military Forces Abroad," 10 Va. J. Int. L. 42 (1969); Reveley, "Presidential War-Making: Constitutional Prerogative or Usurpation?" 55 Va. L. Rev. 1243 (1969). Note, "Congress, the President, and the Power to Commit Forces to Combat," 81 Harv. L. Rev. 1771 (1968); Moore, "The National Executive and the Use of Force Abroad," in J. Moore, Law and the Indo-China War 538 (1972); Mathews, "The Constitutional Power of the President to Conclude International Agreements," 64 Yale L.J. 345, 365 (1955).

39. Moore, *id.* at 544-45. Certain United States Courts of Appeal have taken a similar position, speaking in terms of a requirement of congressional authorization if hostilities are prolonged, or of a certain scale and duration. See Berk v. Laird, 420 F.2d 302 (2d Cir. 1970); Massachusetts v. Laird, 451 F.2d 25 (1st Cir. 1971).

40. Note, "Congress, The President, and the Power to Commit Armed Forces to Combat," *supra* note 38, at 1774-75.

41. E. Corwin, The President: Office and Powers 1787-1957, 4.

42. Corwin gives an anecdote which explains the executive power well. He traces the beginnings of government to a monarch in a forest with absolute plenary power. "At length wearying of his responsibilities, the hypothetical potentate delegated some of them to followers who eventually became 'courts,' and shared others with a more numerous body of subjects who in due time organized themselves into a 'legislature.' The indefinite residuum, called 'executive power,' he kept for himself." *Id.* at 3.

43. See, e.g., J. Locke, Two Treatises of Government, Bk. II, chap. 14, §159, Laslett 2d ed. 392 (1967).

44. Theodore Roosevelt, An Autobiography 406 (1920).

45. Justice Jackson was of the opinion that the executive power clause was not "a grant in bulk of all conceivable executive power." To the contrary, he regarded it "as an allocation to the presidential office of the generic powers thereafter stated." Youngstown Sheet and Tube Co. v. Sawyer, 343 U.S. 579, 641 (1952).

46. W. Taft, Our Chief Magistrate and His Powers, 139-40.

47. 343 U.S. 579 (1952). There was much discussion of this decision. For two excellent articles see Kauper, "The Steel Seizure Case: Congress, The President, and the Supreme Court," 51 Mich. L. Rev. 141 (1952); Corwin, "The Steel Seizure Case: A Judicial Brick without Straw," 53 Col. L. Rev. 53 (1953).

48. 3 M. Farrand (ed.), The Records of the Federal Convention of 1787, 318-19 (rev. ed. 1966).

49. *Supra*, chap. 1 and chap. 5, notes 8 and 9.

50. For this thesis see Note, "Congress, the President, and the Power to Commit Forces to Combat," *supra* note 38, at 1778; see also Reveley, *supra* note 38, at 1285, n. 140. Velvel, *supra* note 37, 454-55 would confine the power to the repelling of sudden attack. Lofgren, *supra* note 37, at 699-700 believes that the founding fathers intended the power to extend only to the repelling of sudden attacks, but that the consensus existing among them as to such a limited view did not last.

51. Note, "Congress, the President, and the Power to Commit Forces to Combat," *id.* at 1779.

52. 11 Annals of Congress: Debates and Proceedings in the Congress of the United States, 1798-1824, 11-2 (1801).

53. No. 1 of "Lucius Crassius" Dec. 17, 1801, Alexander Hamilton and the Founding of the Nation 526 (R. Morris ed. 1957).

54. For a discussion of this evidence and this episode see A. Sofaer, War, Foreign Affairs and Constitutional Power 208 *et seq.* (1976).

55. 5 J. Richardson, Messages and Papers of the President 284 (1917).

56. 67 U.S. (2 Black) 635 (1863).

57. *Id.* at 668-69.

58. *Id.* at 670.

59. Reveley, *supra* note 38 at 1285-86 discusses this presidential power to repel attacks and the power of Congress to repudiate his action.

60. McDougal & Lans, "Treaties and Congressional-Executive or Presidential Agreements: Interchangeable Instruments of National Policy: II," 54 Yale L. J. 534-612-13 (1945); Mathews, *supra* note 38, at 359-65 (1955). But see Berger, *supra* note 37, at 43-44.

61. 2 Moore, A Digest of International Law 412 (1902). See Jennings, "The Caroline and McCleod Cases," 32 Am. J. Int'l L. 82 (1938).

62. Reproduced in Jennings, *id.* at 89. This definition was accepted by the International Military Tribunal at Nuremberg, cmd 6964, p. 28, 1946.

63. See A. V. W. Thomas and A. J. Thomas, Jr., Non-Intervention: The Law and Its Import in the Americas 123 (1956).

64. See W. Beckett, The North Atlantic Treaty 13 (1952); H. Kelsen, Principles of International Law 64 *et seq.* (2d ed. Tucker 1967)).

65. D. Bowett, Self-Defense at International Law, chaps. 9 and 10 (1958); J. Stone, Aggression and World Order, chap. 5 (1958).

66. Bowett, *id.* at 188.

67. *Id.* at 185. See also Stone, supra note 65, at 94-97.

68. B. Cheng, General Principles of International Law as Applied by International Courts and Tribunals 101 (1953).

69. The Address of President Kennedy, "The Soviet Threat to the Americas," is contained in 47 Dept. State Bull. 715-201 (Nov. 12, 1962).

70. Statement of Secretary of State Dean Rusk, at 47 Dept. State Bull., 720-22 (Nov. 12, 1962). But see Chayes, "Law and the Quarantine of Cuba," 41 For. Affairs 550, 554-55 (1962).

71. See, e.g., Bowett, *supra* note 65, chap. 1; Cheng, *supra* note 68, 94 *et seq.*; 1 G. Schwarzenberger, A Manual of International Law 172-73 (4th ed. 1960). The essential rights of a state the violation of which would justify self-defense are, according to Bowett, the following: the right of territorial integrity, the right of political independence, the right of protection over nationals, and certain economic rights. Bowett, *id.* at 270.

72. See A. V. W. Thomas and A. J. Thomas, Jr., The Concept of Aggression 90-92 (1972).

73. See N.Y. Times, Jan. 3, 1975, p. 2, col. 1 where he discussed the fact that a use of force would not be dismissed if it were necessary as a last resort in an emergency.

74. See discussions *supra* at note 56.

75. See discussion *supra* at notes 52, 53, 54 of the two positions.

76. See note 50, *supra.*

77. Reveley, *supra* note 50, at 1287.

78. See Jennings, "The Caroline and McLeod Cases," 32 Am. J. Int'l L. 82, 89 (1938).

79. A. V. W. Thomas and A. J. Thomas, Jr., The Organization of American States 259 (1965).

80. Art. 9, Inter-American Treaty of Reciprocal Assistance, 4 T.I.A.S. 1838 (1970).

81. I. Brownlie, International Law and the Use of Force by States 289 (1963); Bowett, *supra* note 65, at 91-94.

82. Memorandum of the Solicitor of the Department of State, October 5, 1912, Right to Protect Citizens in Foreign Countries by Landing Forces (2d rev. ed. 1929).

83. A. V. W. Thomas & A. J. Thomas, Jr., The Dominican Republic Crisis 1965, 11-18 (Ninth Hammarskjöld Forum, Carey ed. 1967).

84. *Id.*

85. 72 Dept. State Bull. 719-20 (1975); but see Paust, "The Seizure and Recovery of the Mayaguez," 87 Yale L.J. 774-81, 795-803 (1976).

86. Bowett, *supra* note 65, at 100-105.

87. E.g., Bowett, *id.*; Waldock, "The Regulation of the Use of Force by Individual States on International Law," 2 Rec. de Cours 503 (1952).

88. See Memorandum, *supra* note 82.

89. See *supra* note 71.

90. Art. 3, 4 T.I.A.S. 1838 (1970). See also Thomas and Thomas, *supra* note 79, chap. 15.

91. E.g., Vietnam. See U.S. Dept. of State, Office of the Legal Adviser, "The

Legality of United States Participation in the Defense of Viet Nam," 54 Dept. State Bull. 474, 478 (1966).

92. J. Stone, Legal Controls of International Conflict 245 (1954) declares that no right of self-defense exists by reason of an attack upon a third state. See also Kelsen, The Law of the United Nations 792 (1950).

93. For this thesis see Bowett, *supra* note 65, at chap. 10.

94. Bowett, *id.* at 201-2 cites provisions of systems of municipal law which bear out this principle and internationalists who make the analogy.

95. *See* note, "Congress, the President, and the Power to Commit Forces to Combat," *supra* note 38, at 1783.

96. For this thesis see *id.* at 1783-85. Reveley would permit the President to act unilaterally against attacks on United States security interests abroad if delay could not be warranted or if secrecy demanded. Ratification and authorization for the action should be requested of the Congress as soon as possible. Reveley, *supra* note 38, at 7286.

97. See *supra* notes 52, 53, 53, 75 for discussion.

98. 2 U.S.T. 2394 (1951).

99. 4 T.I.A.S. 1838 (1970).

100. See Thomas and Thomas, *supra* note 79 at 261-62.

101. Note, "Congress, the President, and the Power to Commit Forces to Combat," *supra* note 38, at 1783-84.

102. *Id.*

103. Memorandum of Law by Lawyers Committee on American Policy Towards Vietnam, September 1965, as set forth in L. Sohn, Cases on United Nations Law 820, 824 (1967).

104. Memorandum, *supra* note 71.

105. See Corwin, *supra* note 41, chap. 6.

106. The Federalist No. 69, at 460 (Ford ed.).

107. See L. Henkin, Foreign Affairs and the Constitution 53-54 (1972); see also 2 B. Schwartz, A Commentary on the Constitution of the United States, the Powers of Government, the Powers of the President 164 (1963). Schwartz speaks of the use of the Commander-in-Chief power to protect the "external interests" of the United States. Since it is conceded that the President has a broad power over external interests and foreign affairs, he can couple the two powers so as constitutionally to use force abroad without congressional declaration of war.

108. The government has based the President's power upon the foreign relations power, the power to execute the laws, or the right to protect lives of Americans abroad. See Memorandum of the Solicitor, *supra* note 82; J. Rogers, World Policing and the Constitution (1945).

109. See Henkin, *supra* note 107, at 54, 56; 2 Schwartz, *supra* note 107, at 162-64.

110. Wright, The Control of American Foreign Relations 309-10 (1922).

111. 2 Schwartz, supra note 107, at 166; 3 Willoughby, Constitution of the United States 1567 (1929).

112. See, e.g., A. V. W. Thomas and A. J. Thomas, Jr., Non-Intervention: The Law and Its Import in the Americas, chap. 2, "The Era of Intervention in the Americas" (1956).

113. Note, "Congress, the President, and the Power to Commit Forces to Combat," *supra* note 38 at 1774-75, 1787-88. This note speaks of what was known as the neutrality theory, i.e., that congressional approval was not needed when force was used neutrally against a foreign nation (for example, to protect nationals of the intervening state) but that intervention by force into the political life of the foreign state would demand approval by the Congress. And see Wright, *supra* note 110.

114. Thomas and Thomas, *supra* note 112, at 79-97.

115. *Id.* at 91. See also *id.* at 71 for a definition of intervention.

116. Wright, "The Power of the Executive to Use Military Forces Abroad," 10 Va. J. of Int'l L. 43 (1969) states at 49: "The use of force for such political purposes seems to be prohibited by contemporary international law as set forth in the Kellog-Briand Pact, the Nuremberg Charter, and the United Nations Charter. Consequently, this test would require congressional support only if the purpose of the hostility is in violation of international law." Wright goes on to say that several cases suggest that in the use of military action the President must act on a presumption of intention to observe international law unless otherwise authorized by Congress. He cites Miller v. United States, 78 U.S. (11 Wall.) 268 (1871); Mitchell v. Harmony, 54 U.S. (13 How.) 115 (1852); and Fleming v. Page, 50 U.S. (9 How.) 603 (1850).

117. Constitution of the United States of America, Art. II, Sec. 2.

118. It is so stated in the Constitution, Art. VI.

119. 36 U.S. (16 Wall.) 36 (1873).

120. 73 U.S. (6 Wall.) 35 (1868).

121. And see Durand v. Hollins, 4 Blatch. 451, 454 (S.D. N.Y. 1860).

122. See *supra* pp. 51-63.

123. See *infra* pp. 76-79; and see Thomas and Thomas, *supra* note 112, at chap. 14.

124. Respublica v. de Longchamps, 1 Dall. 120, 123 (Pa. Oyer and Terminer, 1784).

125. 175 U.S. 677 (1900).

126. *Id.* at 700.

127. 4 The Works of Alexander Hamilton 444 (Lodge ed. 2d 1903).

128. On the theory that international law is part of the law of the United States, see Dickinson, "The Law of Nations as Part of the National Law of the United States," 101 U. Pa. L. Rev. 26 (1952). Other authority is set forth in L. Henkin, R. Pugh, O. Schachter, H. Smit, International Law, Cases and Materials 116-21 (1980).

129. 135 U.S. 1 (1890).

130. *Id.* at 64.

131. Durand v. Hollins, *supra* note 121. See also Wright, *supra* note 110, at 306.

132. Wright, *id.*

133. Thomas and Thomas, *supra* note 79, at 259.

134. *Id.* at 162-68.

135. Thomas and Thomas, *supra* note 123.

136. Wright, *supra* note 110, at 309.

137. On this proposition see note, "Congress, the President, and the Power to Commit Forces to Combat," *supra* note 38, at 1771, 1787-90.

138. Memorandum of the Solicitor for the Department of State October 5, 1912, Right to Protect Citizens in Foreign Countries by Landing Forces 25 (2d rev. ed. 1929).

139. 51 Dept. State Bull. 838 *et seq.* (1964).

140. On these various uses of force see Memorandum, *supra* note 138; J. Rogers, World Policing and the Constitution (1925).

141. Rogers, *id.* at 58-62.

142. Art. 2, ¶4, U.N. Charter.

143. Art. 51, U.N. Charter; and see *supra* pp. 57-60.

144. Art. 1, ¶ 1, Art. 42 U.N. Charter.

145. See Thomas and Thomas, *supra* note 112, at 130-31.

146. Henkin, *supra* note 107, at 221-22.

147. See Henkin, *id.* at 460.

148. 175 U.S. at 180.

149. *Id.* at 700.
150. The Nereide, 9 Cranch 388, 423 (1815).
151. The Charming Betsey, 2 Cranch 64, 118 (1804).
152. Brown v. United States, 8 Cranch 110, 153 (1814).
153. Henkin, *supra* note 107, at 460.
154. Falk, "International Law and the United States Role in the Viet Nam War," 75 Yale L.J. 1122, 1154-55 (1966).
155. Moore, "International Law and the United States Role in Viet Nam: A Reply," 76 Yale L.J. 1051, 1091-92 (1967).
156. Falk, "International Law and the United States Role in Viet Nam: A Response to Professor Moore," 76 Yale L.J. 1095, 1150 (1967).
157. On political questions see chap. 6.
158. Treaty of Alliance, France 1778, Art. 1, 2 T.I.A. 35 (1931).
159. The text of the treaty is contained in 31 Dept. State. Bull. 899 (1954). President Carter terminated this treaty in 1979. His termination was attacked as unconstitutional. A District Court held that the termination of a treaty must be done by the President with the advice and consent of the Senate or the approval of both houses of Congress. Goldwater v. Carter, 481 F. Supp. 949 (D.D.C. 1979). This judgment was reversed by the Court of Appeals, 617 F.2d 697 (D.C. Cir. 1979). Without decision on the merits, the judgment was voided with instructions to dismiss by the Supreme Court. 62 L. Ed. 2d 428 (1979).
160. 62 Stat., T.I.A.S. 1838, 21 U.N.T.S. 77 (1947).
161. 20 Dept. State Bull. (1949).
162. 31 Dept. State Bull. 393 (1954).
163. *Id.* art. 1.
164. *Supra* note 91.
165. Velvel, *supra* note 37, at 657-58 responds forcefully, stating that even under the treaty the Congress must make the decision to initiate war.
166. 1 Willoughby, The Constitutional Law of the United States 549-52 (2d ed. 1929). Note, "Congress, the President, and the Power to Commit Forces to Combat," *supra* note 38, at 1798-99.
167. Wright, *supra* note 110, at 228-29.
168. 2 B. Schwartz, *supra* note 107, at 182-87. But see Note, "Congress, the President, and the Power to Commit Armed Forces Abroad," *supra* note 38, at 1800.
169. Note, *id.* at 1799 states that collective security treaties have not changed the constitutional power of President and Congress in this regard. See also 2 Schwartz, *id.* at 187-96.
170. *Supra* pp. 51-63.
171. *Id.*
172. 59 Stat. 651 as amended, 63 Stat. 735 (1949); 22 U.S.C. 287d (1976 ed).
173. Resolution of the Security Council, 27 June 1950. S/1511; SCOR, V, Resolutions and Decisions, 1950 (S/INF/4/Rev. 1), p. 5.
174. Resolution of the Security Council, 7 July, S/1588; SCOR, V, Resolutions and Decisions, 1950 (S/INF/5/Rev. 1), p. 5.
175. See 23 Dept. State Bull. 173 et seq. (1950).
176. For varying views concerning Truman's power versus congressional power, see A. Schlesinger, Jr., The Imperial Presidency 130 *et seq.* (1973); Velvel, *supra* note 37 at 455-56; Note, "Congress, the President, and the Power to Commit Forces to Combat," *supra* note 38, at 1792; 2 Schwartz, *supra* note 107, at 190-195.
177. For certain examples see Thomas and Thomas, *supra* note 63, at 21-36; Thomas & Thomas, *supra* note 83, at 24 *et seq.* as well as others.
178. Resolution 377A (V) of the General Assembly, 3 Nov. 1950, GAOR, V, Supp. 20 (A/1775), pp. 10-12.
179. Thomas and Thomas, *supra* note 63, at 172-76.
180. United States v. Belmont Bank, 301 U.S. 324 (1937); United States v.

Pink, 315 U.S. 203 (1942). For comment on the executive agreement power see Henkin, *supra* note 107, at 176-87.

181. At national law they override conflicting state law. United States v. Belmont Bank, *id.* They apparently do not, however, override a previous United States statutory provision. United States v. Guy W. Capps, Inc., 204 F.2d 655 (4th Cir. 1953), *aff'd on other grounds*, 348 U.S. 296 (1955).

182. Wright, *supra* note 116 at 513 outlines the points of criticism.

183. See *supra* pp. 72-79.

184. For discussion of intervention by consent and its legality at international law see Thomas and Thomas, *supra* note 63, at 91-97, 156-68.

185. For intervention in time of civil strife see Thomas and Thomas, *supra* note 79, at 338-45.

186. Thomas and Thomas, *supra* note 63, at 96.

187. See examples set forth in chaps. 2, 3, and 4, *supra.*

188. In the early case of Talbot v. Seeman, 5 U.S. (1 Cranch) 1, 25 (1801) Chief Justice Marshall concluded that a valid congessional authorization of war resulted from congressional action other than a formal declaration; see also Bas v. Tingy, 4 U.S. (4 Dall.) 37, 39, 40-41, 43, 45 (1800). See also, *e.g.*, Orlando v. Laird, 443 F.2d 1039, 1043 (2d Cir. 1971), *cert. denied*, 404 U.S. 869 (1971); Mitchell v. Laird 488 F.2d 611, 615 (D.C. Cir. 1973).

189. National Commitments, Sen. Report No. 797, 90th Cong. 1st Sess. 25 (1967).

190. Mitchell v. Laird, *supra* note 188 at 615.

191. See statements of Undersecretary Katzenbach, U.S. Commitments to Foreign Powers, Hearings Before the Senate Committee For Rel. on S. Res. 151, 90th Cong. 1st Sess., 80-81, 161, 174 (1967). See also Henkin, Foreign Affairs and the Constitution, 333, n. 61 (1972).

192. *Id.* at 82.

193. Note, "Congress, the President, and the Power to Commit Forces to Combat," *supra* note 38, at 1801-2.

194. *Id.*; Moore, *supra* note 38, at 545-48; Velvel, *supra* note 37, at 472-79; Mottola v. Nixon, 318 F. Supp. 538 (N.D. Cal. 1970) rev'd. 464 F.2d 178 (9th Cir. 1972) 464 F.2d 178 (9th Cir. 1972) (Standing).

195. For discussions of the doctrine see generally L. Tribe, American Constitutional Law 284-91 (1978); G. Gunther, Constitutional Law Cases and Materials 407-8 (10th ed. 1980).

196. 69 Stat. 7 (1955).

197. 71 Stat. 5 (1957).

198. 78 Stat. 384 (1964). This resolution was repealed in 1971. 84 Stat. 2053 (1971).

199. Wormuth, *supra* note 37, at 780 *et. seq.*; Note, "Congress, the President, and the Power to Commit Forces to Combat," *supra* note 38, at 1803; Bickel, "Congress, the President, and the Power to Wage War," 48 Chicago Kent L. Rev. 131, 157 (1971). But see Moore, *supra* note 194; Rostow, "Great Cases Make Bad Law," 50 Tex. L. Rev. 833, 885-92 (1972).

200. See, e.g., Yakus v. U.S., 321 U.S. 414 (1944). Outside of the cases involving protection of private rights, the Supreme Court has been liberal in upholding broad delegations of powers. Tribe, American Constitutional Law, 287-91 (1978).

201. 299 U.S. 304 (1936).

202. Wormuth, *supra* note 37, at 796. See Mottola v. Nixon, *supra* note 194, at 545.

203. See *supra* pp. 51-71, 79-87.

204. 443 F.2d at 1042.

205. See, e.g., Velvel, *supra* note 37, at 465-66; Wormuth, *supra* note 37, at

799-807; Strum, "The Supreme Court and the Vietnamese War," 4 Falk, The Vietnam War and International Law 535, at 538-39 (1976).

206. See 2 Schwartz, Commentary on the Constitution of the United States, the Powers of Government 225-26 (1963). See also Velvel, *id*.

207. 360 U.S. 475 (1959).

208. *Id*. at 506-7.

209. Orlando v. Laird, *supra* note 188, at 1042; Berk v. Laird, 429 F.2d 302 at 305; (2d Cir. 1970) Holtzman v. Schlesinger, 484 F.2d 1307, 1309 (2d Cir. 1973). But see Chief Judge Bazelon's opinion in Mitchell v. Laird, 488 F.2d 611, 615 (2d Cir. 1973).

210. Fleming v. Mohawk Wrecking and Lumber Co., 331 U.S. (1) (1947) supports the view that a congressional appropriation may supply the needed ratification of presidential action taken under the war power. Nevertheless, Ex Parte Endo, 323 U.S. 283 (1944), denied that an appropriation act ratified all the activities encompassed by the appropriation. Justice Douglas was of the opinion that the appropriation must plainly show a purpose to bestow the precise authority which is claimed. "We can hardly deduce such a purpose . . . here where a lump sum appropriation was made for the overall program of the authority and no sums were earmarked for the single phase of the total program which is here involved." *Id*. at 303.

211. Strum, *supra* note 205, at 538-39; Velvel, *supra* note 37, at 465-66; note, Congress, the President, and the Power to Commit Forces to Combat, *supra* note 38, at 1801.

212. 418 F.2d 615.

213. See *supra* chap. 6 on Political Question at note 58.

CHAPTER SEVEN

1. 5 U.S. (1 Cranch) 137 (1803).

2. U.S. Const., Art. 3, § 1. In the same opinion Marshall went on to say, however, that the President was "invested with certain political powers, in the exercise of which he is to use his own discretion, and is accountable only to his country in his political character and to his own conscience." 5 U.S. at 165-66.

3. An extensive literature on the doctrine of political question exists. A sample of general studies follows: Field, "The Doctrine of Political Questions in the Federal Courts," 8 Minn. L. Rev. 485 (1924); Finkelstein, "Judicial Self-Limitation," 37 Harv. L. Rev. 338 (1924); Finkelstein, "Further Notes on Judicial Self-Limitation," 39 Harv. L. Rev. 221 (1925); C. Post, The Supreme Court and Political Questions (1936); Tigar, "Judicial Power, the 'Political Question Doctrine,' and Foreign Relations," 17 U.C.L.A. L. Rev. 1135 (1970); Scharpf, "Judicial Review and the Political Question: A Functional Analysis," 75 Yale L.J. 518 (1966); Strum, The Supreme Court and "Political Questions:" A Study in Judicial Evasion (1974); Henkin, "Is There a Political Question Doctrine?" 85 Yale L.J. 597 (1976).

4. L. Tribe, American Constitutional Law 71 (1978).

5. L. Henkin, Foreign Affairs and the Constitution 210 (1972). Schwartz and McCormack, in an article entitled "The Justiciability of Legal Objections to the American Military Effort in Vietnam," 56 Tex. L. Rev. 1033, 1042 (1968), say that the term "political question" is just a label which the courts apply *after* decision is made that the matter at issue should be left to the sole determination by a political department. Another writer says that there is in reality no such thing as a political question. It is only "a cluster of disparate legal rules." Tigar, *supra* note 3, at 1135.

6. Field, *supra* note 3, at 512. And see Scharpf, *supra* note 3, at 555-58.

7. For juridical versus political disputes at international law see A. V. W. Thomas and A. J. Thomas, Jr., The Organization of American States 291-92 (1963).

8. Wechsler, "Toward Neutral Principles of Constitutional Law," 73 Harv. L. Rev. 1, 1-9 (1959).

9. A. Bickel, The Least Dangerous Branch 69-71 (1962); Scharpf, *supra* note 3, at 566-97. Professor Tribe believes that the doctrine rests upon the competence of the court to decide constitutional questions and enforce constitutional rights at issue. Tribe, *supra* note 4, at 79. See also Moore, "The Justiciability of Challenges to the Use of Force Abroad," 10 Va. J. Int'l L. 85 (1969), 3 Falk ed., The Vietnam War and International Law 631 (1972), for a discussion of the functional approach.

10. Henkin, *supra* note 5, at 210-16; Henkin, "Viet-Nam in the Courts of the United States: 'Political Questions,' " 63 Am. J. Int'l L. 284 (1969). This is what the court did in The Prize Cases, 67 U.S. (2 Black) 635 (1863). For discussion see *supra*, chap. 5, notes 28, 57, and *infra* at note 32.

11. 369 U.S. 186 (1962).

12. *Id.*

13. *Id.* at 210.

14. *Id.* at 217.

15. See Tribe, *supra* note 4, at 72, n. 1; G. Gunther, Constitutional Law, Cases & Materials 1688-89 (10th ed. 1980). But see Da Costa v. Laird, 471 F.2d 1146, 1152-54 (2d Cir. 1973), where the court is of the belief that the only strand which permits abstention because of a political question is the constitutional strand, and, that therefore the court has no discretion to refuse to hear the case on, for example, prudential grounds.

16. Strum, *supra* note 3, points out at 63 that a court can always find a textually demonstrable commitment or even a judicially manageable standard if it so desired, or if its desires are otherwise it can fail to find the commitment or standard.

17. 396 U.S. 486 (1969).

18. Wechsler, *supra* note 8, at 8.

19. For excellent discussion of the commitment problem see Scharpf, *supra* note 3, at 538-48.

20. 369 U.S. at 211.

21. But see language in the Prize Cases, *supra* note 10, and In re Neagle, 135 U.S. 1 (1980), which would indicate otherwise. These two cases are discussed *supra* chap. 5, notes 28, 57, 129; Strum, "The Supreme Court and the Vietnamese War," 3 Falk ed., The Vietnam War and International Law 536 (1976) presents at 560-64 interesting thoughts on the reasons behind the Supreme Court's abstention and refusal to decide the issue of the legality of that war as well as its failure to designate the issue a political question.

22. See, e.g., Massachusetts v. Laird, 451 F.2d 26 (1st Cir. 1971). See also Velvel, "The War in Viet Nam: Unconstitutional, Justiciable, and Jurisdictionally Attackable," 16 Kan. L. Rev. 449, at 482 (1968); Moore, *supra* note 9, 3 Vietnam War and International Law at 638-40.

23. Velvel, *id.* at 481; see also Berk v. Laird, 429 F.2d 302 (2d Cir. 1970).

24. Velvel, *id.* at 482.

25. See, e.g., The Pocket Veto Case, 279 U.S. 655 (1929); Missouri Pacific Railroad v. Kansas, 248 U.S. 276 (1919); United States v. Belmont, 301 U.S. 324 (1937); Missouri v. Holland, 252 U.S. 416 (1920); Ex Parte Milligan, 71 U.S. (4 Wall.) 2 (1866). This has been particularly true when personal rights are involved. See Reid v. Covert, 354 U.S. 1 (1957); Korematsu v. United States, 323 U.S. 214 (1944). Schwartz and McCormack, *supra* note 9, at 1041-45 point out that the two basic issues in the Vietnam conflict were the constitutionality of the use of force there without congressional authorization and the violation of treaty obligations. There were said to be questions of construction and interpretation which the court had long considered to be outside the realm of the political question.

26. 343 U.S. 579 (1952).

27. Coleman v. Miller, 307 U.S. 433 (1939).

28. Luther v. Borden, 7 How. 1 (1849); Pacific States Telephone & Telegraph Co. v. Oregon, 233 U.S. 118 (1912).

29. 444 U.S. 996 (1979).

30. U.N. Charter, Art. 2(4), Art. 50.

31. Moore, *supra* note 9, 3 Falk, Vietnam War and International Law at 637-38, 649-52. See also Schwartz & McCormack, *supra* note 5, at 1033-37, 1040; Mitchell v. United States, 386 U.S. 972 (1967) (Douglas, J., dissenting from a denial of certiorari).

32. Moore, id. at 643-45; Schwartz & McCormack, *supra* note 5, at 1042; Henkin, *supra* note 5; Tigar, *supra* note 3, at 1155-57.

33. *Supra* note 10. Justice Brennan in Goldwater v. Carter was the only justice reaching the merits. Four justices abstained on the ground of political question. Justice Brennan believed that the case was justiciable and that no political question was involved, but at the same time he set forth the opinion that the President was constitutionally alone empowered to act to terminate the treaty with Taiwan through his power of recognition and withdrawal thereof.

34. 451 F.2d 26 (1st Cir. 1971).

35. 4 U.S. (4 Dall.) 36 (1800).

36. 451 F.2d at 33.

37. *Id.* at 34.

38. Gunther, *supra* note 15, at 1690-94; W. Lockhart, Y. Kamisar, J. Choper, Constitutional Law Cases-Comments-Questions 47-49 (5th ed. 1980); Moore, *supra* note 9, 3 Vietnam War and International Law, at 634-38; Scharpf, *supra* note 3, at 566-73.

39. Gunther, *id.* at 1688.

40. 307 U.S. 433 (1939).

41. *Id.* at 453-54.

42. 444 U.S. at 997.

43. 400 U.S. 886 (1970).

44. *Id.* at 893.

45. Wallace, in "The War-Making Powers: A Constitutional Flaw," 57 Cornell L. Rev. 719 (1972), points out that the war powers are essentially and inherently of a political nature which makes them difficult if not impossible to bring within the control of the judiciary. See also Scharpf, *supra* note 3, at 567.

46. 62 L. Ed. 2d 428 at 432-33 (1979).

47. Velvel, *supra* note 22, at 479-80.

48. *Id.* at 481-82.

49. 429 F.2d 302 (2d Cir. 1970). Several cases dealing with the question were decided by the Second Circuit. They are excellently discussed by Wenner, "The Indochina War Cases in the United States Court of Appeals of the Second Circuit," 7 N.Y. Univ. J. of Int'l L. & Politics 137 (1974).

50. *Id.* at 305.

51. Velvel, *supra* note 22, at 481.

52. On problems bound up with the right of self-defense see Thomas and Thomas, *supra* note 7, at 249-60.

53. Moore, *supra* note 9 at 92-96.

54. Curtiss-Wright Export Corp. v. United States, 299 U.S. 304 (1936).

55. Strum, *supra* note 21, at 560 is of the opinion that it was more than probable that the President would have disregarded any injunction from the Supreme Court calling the Vietnamese conflict illegal and attempting to terminate hostilities.

56. 443 F.2d 1039 (2d Cir. 1971), cert. denied, 405 U.S. 979 (1972).

57. *Id.* at 1042.

58. *Id.* at 1043.

59. 471 F.2d 1146 (2d Cir. 1973). A previous case had before it the contention that the repeal of the Gulf of Tonkin Resolution by the Congress removed legislative participation in the war and thus made it unconstitutional. The court was of the opinion that even with such repeal there was legislative action showing mutual executive-congressional participation. DaCosta v. Laird, 448 F.2d 1368 (2d Cir. 1971), cert. denied, 405 U.S. 979 (1972).

60. 471 F.2d at 1155.

61. *Id.*

62. 484 F.2d 1307 (2d Cir. 1973).

63. 361 F. Supp. 553 (E.D. N.Y. 1973). The United States Court of Appeals granted a stay of the District Court's judgment pending appeal. Justice Marshall refused an application to vacate the stay. 414 U.S. 1304 (1973); Justice Douglas granted a re-application to vacate the stay. 414 U.S. 1316 (1973). Justice Marshall after polling other members of the court, overruled Douglas's order. 414 U.S. 1321 (1973).

64. 484 F.2d at 1310.

65. But see Schwartz and McCormack, *supra* note 5, at 1047-48 who claim that the institutional framework as in Baker v. Carr is not capable of correcting what they believe to be the unconstitutional usurpation by the President. The potential interplay between the departments is impaired. The executive denies to the Congress its constitutional power to declare war. After the initiation of hostilities, patriotism and loyalty prevent the members of Congress from cutting off funds or taking other action to end the fighting. Thus if there is no judicial intervention the constitutional infringement will continue.

66. See *supra* notes 10 and 32, 33.

67. See Schwartz and McCormack, *supra* note 5, at 1043-45; see also Scharpf, *supra* note 3, at 541-48, but see his discussion at 573-75.

68. As to differing meanings and content of such norms, see Moore, *supra* note 9; 3 Falk ed., Vietnam War and International Law, at 645-46; Moore, "The Control of Foreign Intervention in Internal Conflict," 9 Va. J. Int'l L. 205 (1969); A. V. W. Thomas and A. J. Thomas, Jr., The Concept of Aggression (1972); A. V. W. Thomas and A. J. Thomas, Jr., Non-Intervention: The Law and Its Import in the Americas (1956); Thomas and Thomas, *supra* note 52.

69. Moore, *id.* at 647-48.

70. Strum, *supra* note 3, at 63.

71. Velvel, *supra* note 22, at 483.

72. 400 U.S. at 894.

73. Velvel, *supra* note 22, at 483.

74. *Id.* at 483-84.

75. Strum, *supra* note 3.

76. Velvel, *supra* note 22, at 484-85; Schwartz and McCormack, *supra* note 5, at 1050.

77. Velvel, *id.*; Schwartz and McCormack, *id.*

78. Velvel, *id.*; Schwartz and McCormack, *id.* at 1052-53 point out that a court calling the use of force illegal could be mitigated by the type of decree which the court might render. A court ultimatum to get the troops out would not be necessary. To the contrary, the court could use its equity powers to call upon the military to end the conflict with all deliberate speed, as it did with respect to school segregation in Brown v. Board of Education, 349 U.S. 294 (1955). Nevertheless, some court involvement would be necessary and such involvement and supervision in the winding down of foreign fighting would hardly seem to be within the province of the judiciary.

79. Henkin, "Viet-Nam in the Courts of the United States," *supra* note 10 at 289.

80. Velvel, *supra* note 22, at 484.

81. See Moore, *supra* note 9, Falk ed., Vietnam War and International Law at 640-41, 646-47.

82. *Id.* at 648-49.

83. See, e.g., Atlee v. Baird, 347 F. Supp. 689 (E.D. Pa. 1972), legality of Vietnam War held non-justiciable, aff'd. 411 U.S. 911 (1973); Holtzman v. Schlesinger, *supra* notes 62, 63; Orlando v. Laird, *supra* note 56; and others.

84. See, e.g., Moore, *supra* note 9, Falk ed. Vietnam War and International Law at 633-38.

85. His statement in Colegrove v. Green, 328 U.S. 549, 556 (1946).

86. *Supra* note 34.

87. *Supra* notes 49, 56, 59, 69.

88. On these requirements in general see Tribe, *supra* note 4, at 60-62, 79-114; Nowak, Rotunda, Young, Constitutional Law 64-83 (1978).

89. Warth v. Seldin, 422 U.S. 490, 499 (1975).

90. Gunther, *supra* note 15, at 1655-63.

91. Berk v. Laird, 429 F.2d 302, 306 (2d Cir. 1970). See also Orlando v. Laird, *supra* note 49; Massachusetts v. Laird, *supra* note 33.

92. See Berk v. Laird, *id.*; Mottola v. Nixon, 318 F. Supp. 538, 547 n. 12 (N.D. Cal. 1972); reversed 464 F.2d 178 (9th Cir. 1972). See also Schwartz and McCormack, *supra* note 5, at 705.

93. Ashton v. United States, 404 F.2d 95 (8th Cir. 1968), cert. denied 394 U.S. 960 (1969).

94. United States v. Mitchell, 369 F.2d 323 (2d Cir. 1966), cert. denied, 386 U.S. 972 (1967).

95. 464 F.2d 178 (9th Cir. 1972).

96. 451 F.2d 26 at 29.

97. 262 U.S. 447 (1923).

98. 400 U.S. 886 at 887-91 (1970).

99. 488 F.2d 611 (1973).

100. *Id.* at 613.

101. *Id.*

102. *Id.* at 614.

103. See Note, "Congressional Access to the Federal Courts," 90 How. L. Rev. 1632 at 1638 (1977). Herein it is pointed out that the court has granted restricted access to the suits of members of Congress permitting standing to only a few interests, such as the protection of their votes for upcoming legislation and their rights to engage in debates. And see Holtzman v. Schlesinger, *infra* note 105, where the court reached opposite conclusion on this point.

104. 484 F.2d 1307 (2d Cir. 1973).

105. *Id.* at 1315.

106. 392 U.S. 83 (1968).

107. 415 F.2d 236 (10th Cir. 1969), *cert. denied,* 396 U.S. 1042 (1970).

108. District Judge Sweigert, in Mottola v. Nixon, *supra* note 92.

109. 471 F.2d at 1150.

110. 339 U.S. 763.

111. 418 U.S. 208 (1974).

112. On the doctrine of sovereign immunity as applicable to the federal government, see 1 B. Schwartz, A Commentary on the Constitution of the United States: The Powers of Government 404-9 (1963).

CHAPTER EIGHT

1. See *supra* pp. 49-51.

2. 16 American Jurisprudence 264-70 (1964). See also Shurtleff v. U.S. 189 U.S. 311 at 316 (1903) where the Supreme Court upheld presidential action on

the basis that it had been the universal practice of the President, uncontested by Congress "for over a century." See also Justice Frankfurter's opinion in Youngstown Sheet & Tube Co. v. Sawyer. 343 U.S. 579 at 610-11 (1952).

3. 15 Stat. 223 (1868); 22 U.S.C. 1732 (1970).

4. See *supra* pp. 5-6, 51.

5. A. V. W. Thomas and A. J. Thomas, Jr., Non-Intervention: The Law and Its Import in the Americas 79-91 (1956).

6. See *supra* chaps. 2, 3, 4, 5.

7. Nobleman, "Financial Aspects of Congressional Participation in Foreign Relations," 289 Annals 145 at 154 (1953).

8. Chap. 720, Sec. 3(e), 54 Stat. 885 (1940); Merlo Pusey, The Ways We Go to War 74 (1971).

9. See *supra* pp. 51-52.

10. NATO Treaty, 43 A.J.I.L. Supp. pp. 159-62 (1949).

11. Senate Committee on Foreign Relations, "War Powers," Senate Rep. No. 92-606, 92nd Congress, 2nd Sess., pp. 30-34 (1972).

12. See *supra* pp. 51 *et seq.*

13. Senate Report #797, 90th Cong. 1st Sess. 25, 1967.

14. N.Y. Times June 26, 1969. Congressional Quarterly, 3 Congress & the Nation 1969-1972, p. 857 (1973).

15. N.Y. Times, Dec. 16, 1969.

16. 116 Cong. Rec. 37398-37408 (1970).

17. Weekly Comp. Press. Doc. VI 597, 1970.

18. Staff of Senate Comm. on Foreign Relations 91st Cong., 2nd Sess., Documents Relating to the War Powers of Congress, the President's Authority as Commander-in-Chief & the War in Indo-China, 182 Comm. Print, Statement of W. H. Rehnquist, 1970.

19. N.Y. Times, July 1, 1970.

20. N.Y. Times, July 10, 1970.

21. S. Con. Res. 64, N.Y. Times, July 11, 1970.

22. N.Y. Times, Jan. 1, 1971.

23. N.Y. Times, July 2, 1970.

24. Sec. 12, 84 Stat. 2055, 1971.

25. N.Y. Times, Jan. 1, 1971.

26. H. Truman, Memoirs, Years of Trial and Hope, 478 (1956).

27. N.Y. Times, May 3, 1970; N.Y. Times, Sept. 1, 1970; N.Y. Times, Sept. 2, 1970.

28. Cong. Quarterly Inc., 3 Congress & the Nation 1969-1972 pp. 12-13; 917-19 (1973).

29. N.Y. Times, Sept. 22, 1971.

30. In the defense procurement authorization bill the wording of the Mansfield amendment was changed from being the "sense of Congress" to the "policy of the United States." In signing the bill Nixon stated,

To avoid any possible misconceptions, I wish to emphasize that Section 601 of this Act—the so-called Mansfield amendment—does not represent the policies of this administration. Section 601 urges that the President establish a "final date" for the withdrawal of all U.S. forces from Indochina, subject only to the release of U.S. prisoners of war and an accounting for the missing in action. Section 601 expresses a judgment about the manner in which the American involvement in the war should be ended.

However, it is without binding force or effect and it does not reflect my judgment about the way in which the war should be brought to a conclusion. My signing of the bill that contains this section, therefore, will not change the policies I have pursued and that I shall continue to pursue toward this end. [N.Y. Times, Nov. 14, 1971.]

31. N.Y. Times, Dec. 18, 1971.

32. 3 Congress & Nation, *supra* note 28 at 849 (1973).

33. *Id.*, N.Y. Times, Apr. 13, 1972.

34. *Id.*

35. C.Q. Guide, Current American Government, Spring 1973, p. 39 (1973).

36. N.Y. Times, Dec. 19, 1972.

37. N.Y. Times, Jan. 28, 1973.

38. N.Y. Times, Mar. 30, 1977.

39. N.Y. Times, Feb. 22, 1973.

40. H.R. 7447.

41. N.Y. Times, June 27, 1973.

42. H.R. 9055; H. Rep. 93 350 (1973).

43. N.Y. Times, June 27, 1973.

44. Public Law 93-50, N.Y. Times, July 2, 1973.

45. See *supra* pp. 103-4.

46. 119 Cong. Rec. 24653-24708 (1973).

47. 119 Cong. Rec. 25051-25120 (1973).

48. *Id.*

49. N.Y. Times, Oct. 5, 1973; H. Rept. 93-547.

50. N.Y. Times, Oct. 11, 12, 13 (1973).

51. Public Papers of Pres. 893-1973 N.Y. Times October 25, 1973.

52. H. J. Res. 542-PL 93-148. N.Y. Times, Nov. 8, 1973.

53. ". . . it can only be said that their [the Framers'] intentions cannot be accurately ascertained. They were a brilliant and contentious group. Some thought this; others that; and it will never be entirely clear when the final collective judgment came to rest." Richard Funston, A Vital National Seminar—The Supreme Court in American Political Life 11 (1978).

54. 4 Blatch 451, 454 (1860).

55. Corwin, The President: Office & Powers (4th ed. 1964); Charles Black, "The Working Balance of the American Political Departments," 1 Hastings Constitutional Law Quarterly 18 (1974).

56. Theodore C. Sorensen, Kennedy 702 (1965).

57. Findlay, War Powers: a Test of Compliance, Hearings Before the House Committee on International Relations, 94th Cong., 1st Sess. 91, 1975.

58. 123 Cong. Rec. S11319, Daily Ed. June 30, 1977.

59. N.Y. Times, Apr. 21, 1977. See also Findlay, note 76 at 57.

60. The War Powers Resolution: Relevant Documents, Subcommittee on International Security & Scientific Affairs of the House Committee on International Relations. 94th Congress, 1st Session. Comm. Pub. 1975 pp. 13-14.

61. N.Y. Times, Mar. 19, 1981.

62. H. Report #547, 93rd Cong., 1st Sess. 8-1973.

63. 119 Cong. Rec. H9643 daily ed. Nov. 7, 1973.

64. 119 Cong. Rec. H9648, daily ed. Nov. 7, 1973.

65. Findlay, *supra* note 57 at 91.

66. Report dated April 4, 1975, from President Gerald R. Ford to Hon. Carl Albert, Speaker of the House of Representatives in Compliance with Section 4 of the War Powers Resolution set forth in Subcommittee on International Security & Scientific Affairs of the House of Representatives Committee on International Relations, 94th Cong., 1st Sess. "The War Powers Resolution Relevant Documents" Com. Print at p. 7. (Hereafter cited as "Relevant Docs.")

67. *Id.* at 6.

68. Weekly Com. Pres. Doc. XI 363, Apr. 10, 1976.

69. H. Doc. #105, 124, 94th Cong. 1st Sess. 1975.

70. 121 Cong. Rec. H. 3540-3551 Daily ed. May 1, 1978.

71. Report dated April 30, 1975, from President Gerald R. Ford to Hon. Carl Albert, Speaker of the House of Representatives, in compliance with Section 4(a)(2) of the War Powers resolution (Relevant Docs. note 85) at 14.

72. War Powers: A Test of Compliance, Hearings Before the Subcommittee on International Security & Scientific Affairs of the House Comm. on Int'l. Relations, 94th Cong., 1st Sess. 85 (1975).

73. *Id.* at 3.

74. Report Dated May 15, 1975, From President Gerald R. Ford to Hon. Carl Albert, Speaker of the House of Representatives, *id.* at 76.

75. N.Y. Times, May 16, 1975.

76. *Id.*

77. Test of Compliance, *supra* note 57, pp. 77-78.

78. N.Y. Times, May 16, 1975.

79. Test of Compliance, *supra* note 57, at 77-78.

80. N.Y. Times, June 5, 1975.

81. Relevant Doc., *supra* note 66, at 18; Test of Compliance, *supra* note 57, at 76.

82. N.Y. Times, May 16, 17, 18, 1975.

83. 121 Congress. Rec. S. 8825-8828, Daily Ed. May 21, 1975.

84. N.Y. Times, Mar. 6, 1977.

85. A. J. Schweppe, "World Court Rulings: Iran," 14 The International Lawyer 529 (1980).

86. N.Y. Times, Apr. 25, 26, 1980; Time, Oct. 18, 1982.

87. *Id.*

88. West Publishing Co., U.S. Code Congressional-Administrative News. 96th Congress, 2nd Sess. June 1980 "Operation to Rescue the American Hostages Held in Iran," p. 1525.

89. *Id.* at 1527.

90. N.Y. Times, Sept. 30, 1982.

INDEX